THE BLOO□ [barcode: CW00531148] ⌐ES

THE BLOOD AND THE BLUES

Daring Escapes, Dangerous *Songs*: The Legacy of SLAVERY'S Underground Railroad

Danny Smith

with Bill Hampson

Foreword by Jessy Dixon

Authentic

MILTON KEYNES ● COLORADO SPRINGS ● HYDERABAD

13 12 11 10 09   7 6 5 4 3 2 1

First published in 2009 by Authentic Media
9 Holdom Avenue, Bletchley, Milton Keynes, Bucks, MK1 1QR
1820 Jet Stream Drive, Colorado Springs, CO 80921, USA
Medchal Road, Jeedimetla Village,
Secunderabad 500 055, A.P., India
www.authenticmedia.co.uk

Authentic Media is a division of IBS-STL U.K., limited by
guarantee, with its Registered Office at Kingstown Broadway,
Carlisle, Cumbria, CA3 0HA. Registered in England & Wales No.
1216232. Registered charity 270162

British Library Cataloguing in Publication Data

A catalogue record for this book is available from
the British Library

ISBN-13: 978-1-86024-709-5

Cover design by fourninezero design.
Print Management by Adare
Printed in Great Britain by J.H. Haynes and Co., Sparkford

To Jessica

Dedication and Thanks

This book is dedicated to my beloved daughter Jessica who passed away, tragically, suddenly, on 27 December 2007. She was twenty-two. Her loss in my life is indescribable. She was such a complete part of my world that nothing can ever be the same again. Jessie was the first to read an early draft of this book, and, soon afterwards, she said to me, 'Dad, make sure that my name is in your book.' Of course, I always expected to name Jess in these pages. Just not this way.

Joan, Rachel, Luke, Mum and Clement – your enduring love warms my heart. Matt Newman, the affection and care you express for Rachel is such an encouragement.

Our friends everywhere shared this winter season with us; I thank each of you, though only a few are named here: Janet and Craig Rickards, Father Shay Cullen, Hazel Thompson, George Verwer, Roley Horowitz, Wanno Hanoveld, Dr Wai Sin Hu, Dirk Jan Groot, Bernadette Charehwa, Ann Buwalda, Revd K.K. Devaraj, Shoba and Sandesh Kaddam, David Alton, Sam Yeghnazar, Katie and Guy Thomas, Charlotte Saunders, Ryan Dhillon, Aninha Capaldi, Lois Brown, Rosemary Matthews, Frank and Marlene Rice, Rajiv Hanspal,

Fiona Castle, Chacko Thomas, Mark Rowland, Ian Andrews, Rosemary Morris, Alice and Paul Diamond, Christine and Keith Lock, Mathilda and David Armstrong and Jim and Kitty Thompson.

And finally, thanks to Bill Hampson, who had the vision for this book. He has been such an encouraging figure, from our first encounter in 1981 when he was a prime mover in the Campaign to Free the Siberian Seven, to Pam for her encouragement and Ali Hull, who helped bring it through.

For Jess

We decided to remember Jessica by celebrating her life and have set up a charitable tribute to her in countries she loved and intended to return to. In the Philippines, Fr Shay Cullen established The Jessica Smith Memorial Scholarship Fund to help with the education of trafficked, exploited and under-privileged children. In India, we will help to fund a home for orphaned and abandoned children from Bombay's sex industry run by Bombay Teen Challenge and to pay the salary of workers who rescue Children at Risk. In Zimbabwe, Jess's friends have formed a charity, Jessica's House, working in close cooperation with churches and local authorities. This is a simple but effective response to the HIV/AIDS crisis crippling Zimbabwe today. It includes a home for orphans and vulnerable children; a foster-care programme in the community and an HIV/AIDS awareness campaign in the community.

Danny Smith

Jessica's Tribute will be operated by Jubilee Campaign. Contact us for more information:

Jubilee Campaign, PO Box 700, Addlestone, Surrey, KT15 9BW Tel 01 200 430430
info@jubileecampaign.co.uk www.jubileecampaign.co.uk

The Epiphany Trust, St David's, Park Road South, Newton-le-Willows, Merseyside, WA12 8EY. Tel 01925 220999 or bill@epiphany.org.uk www.epiphany.org.uk.

Sincere thanks to all who have helped on this book by researching, typing, checking and encouraging, particularly Pam Gilligan, Sharon Noon, Yolande Burtonwood, Gill Dickinson, Jessy Dixon, Dave Bruce, Kevin Dillon, Micah Hampson, Francis Davis, and Ali Hull, without whom it wouldn't have happened.

Thanks also to the Epiphany Trustees: Robert Song, Barbara Mace, Ken Hargreaves and David Kay for giving me their total support, and especially my wife Pam who is always my best encourager.

Bill Hampson

Contents

Foreword

Jessy Dixon

The Blood and the Blues is a 'must read' for everyone. It is a book I truly couldn't put down. I am especially excited about it because, when travelling around the world, singing in around one hundred and fifty concerts every year, I often introduce myself to an audience by telling them, 'I'm from Chicago, the home of Al Capone, Oprah Winfrey, Michael Jordan . . . and Jessy Dixon.'

To say I'm from Chicago is close enough for an audience in Oklahoma or Oslo, London or Lagos, but I really live in the small country town of Crete, Illinois, two hours drive from downtown Chicago.

Recently, whilst researching the songs of the 'Underground Railroad' for a new album, I was surprised to discover that Crete was one of the Underground Railroad's most important stations. I was amazed at the enormous role that my home town of the last twenty years played in the history of slavery.

The Blood and the Blues came to my attention and, after reading it, I was hooked. It enabled me to better understand the heroism of those people who, two hundred years ago, were members of the Underground Railroad.

And for those who, like myself, have an interest in the music that emerged during that period and that has had such a massive impact on the music played and listened to by every generation since, *The Blood and the Blues* is essential reading.

Introduction

Bill Hampson

The stories of how enslaved Africans in the Southern states of America escaped the oppression of slavery have captivated people for many years. Their experiences were thrilling and daring; they faced overwhelming odds with courage and ingenuity; many of their audacious exploits carried an assurance of faith and a depth of conviction that goes beyond anything most of us have experienced or could imagine. And yet so many of these true-life adventures have remained hidden and unknown.

> ✦
> The music that emerged from these slave communities was both inspiring and uplifting
> ✦

The music that emerged from these slave communities was both inspiring and uplifting. Their songs and rhythms influenced the music of the period and changed popular music in the West from that time on. All the songs of our age, every song in our pop charts, every one downloaded from iTunes, virtually every song sung by each expectant singer auditioning for *Pop Idol* or

X-Factor has been influenced by the music of the slaves and the rhythms that beat in their hearts as they were chained up on those terrible slaving ships that stole an estimated eleven million people from Africa and carried them to become a slave labour force for the masters of the New World.

Slavery's Early Days

Slavery has existed since the earliest records of civilization. The empires of Egypt, Persia, Greece and Rome were built on slavery, on a massive scale. Throughout the Middle Ages, slavery flourished, particularly in southern Europe and northern Africa. Christians had Muslim slaves in Spain, until the Muslims took over, and then the Christians were enslaved. In the fourteenth century, there were thirty thousand slaves in the Kingdom of Granada.

Transatlantic slavery started with Christopher Columbus, though it was a complete reversal of what was to come: slaves from the Caribbean were sent for sale in Europe. This experiment was a total failure, almost all the slaves died of cold and disease.

The transportation of African slaves to the Caribbean gained momentum early in the sixteenth century with the discovery that the climate was ideal for growing sugar cane. In 1562, Captain John Hawkins 'assured that Negroes were very good merchandise in Hispaniola . . . decided to make a trial thereof'. Queen Elizabeth I gave her approval to the expedition, but expressed the hope that slaves would not be taken against their will. Hawkins's voyage transported three hundred African slaves and, in his own words, 'made a good profit'.

Even so, for the remainder of the sixteenth and the first half of the seventeenth centuries, the trade in slaves remained comparatively small, with about eight thousand slaves a year crossing the Atlantic. It was the burgeoning demand for sugar that transformed the slave trade into a massive industry. As the popularity of coffee, tea and chocolate grew within Europe, so the plantations boomed. For the owners this meant enormous wealth: for the slaves, it led to a severe deterioration in their living and working conditions, as owners pressed for higher and higher profits. By 1667, land prices in Barbados were thirty times higher than they had been twenty years earlier, and in the same period, the number of slaves on the island increased from six thousand to eighty thousand. By the 1730s, Britain had over 150 ships employed in the trade, and that decade saw a great increase in slave traffic to the English colonies on the American mainland – and with it the establishment of Liverpool as Britain's foremost slaving port.

Liverpool had much going for it as a slaving city: it was well positioned for the Atlantic trade, out of the way of the French navy in times of war, and easily able to evade any duty on imported goods by simply landing them on the Isle of Man. The demand for slave ships made Liverpool a world-leader in ship-building, and commercial dynasties were funded by families who invested in the trade. Many of the city's buildings and roads carry the names of these families, including that of slave-trader James Penny, of the Beatles' 'Penny Lane' fame.

In the 1780s, as the abolitionist William Wilberforce began his political career, three quarters of a million people were forcibly transported across the Atlantic, almost half of them in British ships. In the latter years of the eighteenth century, the slave trade was considered by most to be indispensable to Britain's prosperity.

While history rightly credits Wilberforce for his role in the abolition of the slave trade, he was far from alone. Granville Sharp, Thomas Clarkson, freed slave Olaudah Equiano, George Fox and many others less well known, particularly women, worked tirelessly to end this dreadful trade. Amongst those calling for abolition, early on, were a considerable body of British women, from all classes. Mary Birkett, Hannah More and Mary Wollstonecraft were most prominent amongst hundreds of white women who spoke out against the slave trade, boycotted slave-grown produce and wrote anti-slave trade verses to raise awareness of the violation of family life under slavery. When Josiah Wedgwood, the famous potter and abolitionist, produced a ceramic cameo of a kneeling male slave in chains, with the slogan 'Am I Not a Man and a Brother?' women campaigners secured production of a similar brooch, with the caption, 'Am I Not a Woman and a Sister?'

The Underground Railroad

The Underground Railroad was a vast network of people who helped fugitive slaves escape to the Northern states of America. No one individual or organization ran it: rather it was made up of thousands of individuals, many white but most black, who operated mainly in their own localities but still managed to move thousands of slaves northward each year. According to some estimates, the South of the United States lost one hundred thousand slaves between 1810 and 1850.

Organized assistance for runaways began towards the end of the eighteenth century, and around 1831 the system of helping slaves escape was dubbed the Underground Railroad, after the emerging steam railways. Railroad terminology was used: the homes where fugitives would rest and eat were called 'stations' and 'depots' and were run by 'stationmasters'. Those who contributed money or goods were 'stockholders' and the 'conductor' was responsible for moving fugitives from one 'station' to the next.

For the slave, running away was extremely difficult. To actually get off the plantations or away from their owners meant relying almost entirely on their own resources. Sometimes a conductor would enter a plantation and guide the runaway northward. They would move at night, generally travelling between ten and fifteen miles to the next station, where they would rest and eat, hiding in barns and other out of the way places. While they waited, a message would be sent to the next station to alert the stationmaster.

> ✦
> For the slave, running away was extremely difficult
> ✦

For any escape, finance was necessary. New clothes were needed: any black man, woman or child, dressed in tattered clothing, would invariably attract attention. Sometimes it was necessary to buy a ticket for the real railway, or to book a passage on a ship. This money was donated by individuals or raised by groups, including vigilance committees, which sprang up in the larger towns and cities of the North, particularly around Philadelphia and Boston. As well as cash, these organizations provided food and lodging, and helped fugitives find jobs and settle into a community.

Songs of Runaway Slaves

Harriet Tubman, who made many trips to the South after her own escape, and escorted over three hundred slaves to freedom, was one of the first to use songs to pass on messages and instructions. It was forbidden to teach slaves to read or write (although many could do both) but the singing of songs was not forbidden. The seemingly innocent spirituals, as the slave songs came to be known, were more than simple hymns of endurance and a belief in a better after-life. They allowed the slaves to communicate secret messages and information to each other about the Underground Railroad.

The songs were part of a sophisticated system that left no incriminating evidence for the plantation owners to find. Codes within the songs told slaves when, how and where to escape. They also included warnings: 'Wade in the Water', a spiritual that Harriet Tubman often sang to escaping slaves, told them to abandon the paths and move along the rivers, to throw chasing dogs off the scent.

Harriet's favourite spiritual is now the anthem of England's rugby supporters: 'Swing Low, Sweet Chariot'. The chariot is the carriage and wagons used to transport fleeing slaves. As the railways spread, however, the word 'train' replaced the word 'chariot', as shown by the song 'The Gospel Train's A-coming'. 'The Gospel Train' soon became a code name for the Underground Railroad, and when slaves heard this song, they knew that either a conductor was amongst them or that there were fleeing slaves nearby. Another song, 'This Train is Bound for Glory', was connected to the Underground Railroad, with 'glory' meaning freedom, but extra caution was needed when singing train songs, as their imagery was easier for outsiders to interpret than the language of the spirituals had been, with their biblical references.

No song, though, is more closely associated with the Underground Railroad than 'Follow the Drinking

Gourd'. The message of this song is simply to follow the North Star. A drinking gourd was a cup with a long handle, something like a ladle, and similar in shape to the constellation of the Big Dipper in the night sky, the brightest star of which is the North Star.

The song was taught to the slaves by a one-legged sailor, Peg Leg Joe, who worked at various jobs on the plantations as he made his way around the South. At each job, he would befriend the slaves, teaching them the words of the song. His plantation visits focused on the area north of Mobile, Alabama, in the late 1850s and early 1860s. The escape route travelled north to the head of the Tombigbee River, then down the Tennessee to the Ohio River. To guide the slaves along the way, the trail was marked with the outline of a human's left foot, with a round circle in the place of the right foot.

✦
The slave-owners often ridiculed the words sung by the slaves
✦

The slave-owners often ridiculed the words sung by the slaves, not realizing what the words meant, or that their slaves were singing of their pain and their dreams of reaching freedom. The songs also enabled the slaves to preserve a degree of intellectual freedom and a sense of superiority, and the melodies and music were filled with images and ideas remembered from their past. Later, this music was to bring a uniquely original and inspiring contribution to the development of popular music. As Elvis Presley said, 'No one can sing it the way they do.'

The singing was not, however, and despite what many white people fondly believed, a sign of pleasure. Freed slave Frederick Douglass wrote:

> I have been utterly astonished, since I came to the North, to find persons who could speak of the singing among slaves as evidence of their contentment and happiness. I have often sung to drown my sorrow, but seldom to express my happiness. Crying for joy, and singing for joy were alike uncommon to me while in the jaws of slavery. The singing of a man cast away on a desolate island might be as appropriately considered as evidence of contentment and happiness as the singing of a slave; the songs of the one and of the other are prompted by the same emotion.[1]

The songs sung by the slaves brought new words into the English language, words that are now in common usage. Tribes people from West Africa introduced words that quickly gained popularity. The Wolof people, who were frequently used as interpreters by the European slave-traders, were brought to America between 1670 and 1700, and worked mainly as house servants. They are thought to have been the first Africans whose language and culture were absorbed into the emerging American culture. Their word 'Okay' or 'OK' is probably the most commonly used word, worldwide, and was first recorded in the speech of African Americans around 1776.

✦

The songs sung by the slaves brought new words into the English language

✦

During the Jazz era, other Wolof words emerged as American slang and gained in popularity: 'jive' originated from *jey*; 'heop', 'hip' and 'hippie' can be traced to the verb *hipi* which means 'to open one's eyes'. 'Dig' (as in 'Dig this, man!') came from *dega*; 'cat' or 'cool cat' was close to *kai*. The Wolof word for slave was *jaam* giving rise to 'jamboree', a noisy slave celebration, and 'jam' session, which, during the days of plantation slavery, meant a time when enslaved musicians and their friends gathered together.

Other phrases that were borrowed from Wolof include the expression 'to kick the bucket'; 'hulla-baloo'; 'juke' as in jukebox; 'moola' for money; 'sock' (as in 'Sock it to me, baby!'); 'bug' (as in jitterbug); 'bozo' (stupid); 'bogus' and 'be with it' (meaning to be in fashion). 'Banana' was the Wolof word for the fruit and was first recorded in 1563. It entered the main-stream language via Spanish and Portuguese in the seventeenth century.

The Drawbacks of Freedom

To the fugitive slave aboard the Underground Railroad, the North was the land of freedom. Unfortunately, on arriving there, they quickly found out that while they were no longer slaves, they weren't free either. The North had emancipated its slaves, but it was not yet ready to treat them as citizens. While working-class men gained new rights, particularly the right to vote, blacks, Native Americans and women were not included.

By the middle of the nineteenth century, European immigrants were pouring into the North. Most had faced discrimination, some outright persecution, in their native countries. In America they found their rights expanding rapidly. They were now part of a privileged category: they were 'white'.

While class differences and ethnic prejudices existed among white Americans, the bottom line was that no matter how poor or degraded they were, they knew there was a class of people below them. Even the poor-est were considered superior to blacks and Indians, sim-ply by virtue of being white. As a result, most identified with the rest of the white race and defended the institution of slavery. Working class whites did this, even though slavery did not benefit them and was, in many ways, against their best interests.

Before 1800, freed black Americans had nominal rights of citizenship. In some places they could vote, serve on juries and work in skilled trades. But as abolitionist laws were passed in Britain, France and elsewhere in Europe, the need to justify slavery in the Americas grew. Racism became stronger and freed blacks gradually lost their rights. New Jersey took away the black vote in 1807.[2]

In 1857, in the infamous case of Dred Scott v Sandford, the Supreme Court formally declared that blacks were not citizens of the United States.[3]

In the nineteenth century, Northern blacks became frequent targets of mob violence. Homes, churches and schools were looted and burned. Ironically, Philadelphia (the city of brotherly love) was the site of the worst and most frequent mob violence. City officials there generally refused to protect African-Americans, and blamed them for inciting violence, with what was described as their 'uppity' behaviour.

> ✦
> Racisim became stronger and freed blacks gradually lost their rights
> ✦

Together with their white allies, black Americans refused simply to sit back and accept Northern racism. Unwelcome in white institutions, they founded their own churches, schools and orphanages. They created mutual aid societies to provide financial assistance to those in need. They helped fugitive slaves adjust to life in the North and, working together, took legal measures to prevent the erosion of rights and to protest against new restrictions.

'Political change comes over the dead bones of its pioneers,' wrote the late Michael Fogarty, the Christian Democrat writer and activist. Nowhere was that more true than in the USA. While the owning of slaves was eventually abolished in 1865, making the Underground Railroad obsolete, it would be a hundred years before the United States would see real change in the relations between the black and white races.

Even the Second World War brought no improvement. In the 1950s, America was still segregated along racial lines and most African-Americans had not been granted the social freedom they had expected from emancipation. The Jim Crow laws, which called for 'separate but equal' facilities continued to support racial injustice in the fields of housing, education and the vote, and all attempts to repeal the laws met with violent resistance. There were major stand-offs and race riots, notably in Little Rock, Arkansas, in 1954, the year of the Brown v Board of Education Act, which led eventually to the desegregation of schools.

The Civil Rights movement is often said to have started when a black woman, Rosa Parks, refused to give up her seat on a bus to a white person, in 1955. A 381-day bus boycott followed in Montgomery, Alabama, which eventually led to the desegregation of America's buses. The Reverend Martin Luther King rose to prominence as the leader of the Civil Rights movement, and in 1963, following riots in Birmingham, Alabama, led 125,000 protestors through Detroit on the 'Great March for Freedom'.

Like the Underground Railroad, the struggles of the Civil Rights movement were accompanied by songs to encourage, direct and inspire those on the road to freedom. Equal rights would no doubt have been won without the participation of Blues, Gospel and Folk singers, but the

songs helped massively. Thousands were written and performed. Pete Seeger's song, 'We Shall Overcome', has been
sung since at almost every struggle where people have
stood up for their rights, but it was particularly inspira-
tional to the Civil Rights movement because of its deep
roots in the African-American community. Another song
that raised the most fundamental Civil Rights issue was
Bob Dylan's 'Blowing in the Wind', which was first made
famous by folk singers Peter, Paul and Mary, and which
asked what made a man worthy to be called a man.

Music was to receive a huge popular boost with the
advent of Motown. Berry Gordy who, like one and a half
million other African-Americans, had left the impoverished
rural South to seek better opportunities in the industrial
North, created a music business that evolved into Motown
Records. Inspired by the
assembly line at the Ford factory where he worked, Gordy
aimed to create a 'hit factory'
where 'a kid off the street
could walk in one door and
come out another a recording
artist – a star'. The Supremes,
Stevie Wonder, Marvin Gaye, The Four Tops and many
others soon became the embodiment of this vision.

> ✦
> **Music was to receive a
> huge popular boost
> with the advent of
> Motown**
> ✦

Gospel music was also significant. Strongly influenced by Thomas Dorsey, who was recognized by all as
the 'Father of Gospel Music', the songs of Mahalia
Jackson, Sam Cooke, James Cleveland and the Staples
Sisters became synonymous with the Civil Rights movement. Ray Charles, Aretha Franklin and Wilson Pickett
all started their careers singing Gospel and a teenage
Jessy Dixon, now having taken up James Cleveland's
mantle as 'King of Gospel', wrote 'Trouble Don't Last
Always' for a Martin Luther King rally.

The Staples Sisters's 'When Will We Be Paid for the Work We've Done?' brings together the whole of African-American history up to that point, including slavery, the construction of the roads and the railways, and demands payment and reparation for the exploitation that has been suffered by the black community. Arguably the most popular song of the slave liberation movement of the 1860s became the anthem of the Civil Rights movement of the 1960s: 'We Shall Not be Moved'. Like many great protest songs, it sings of the refusal to bow to the powers that be and the importance of standing up for what you believe in.

The Civil Rights movement also revived traditional spirituals, songs like 'This Little Light of Mine' and 'Oh, Freedom', which was performed by Joan Baez on 28 August 1963, prior to Martin Luther King's 'I have a dream' speech. In 1968, using the same biblical language as Harriet Tubman's spirituals, Dr King made one of his most important and inspiring speeches: 'I've been to the mountain top . . . and I've looked over, and I've seen the Promised Land.' Twenty-four hours later, he was shot dead at the Lorraine Motel in Memphis, Tennessee.

With the renewed interest in the slave trade and the campaigns that ended it, coupled with the 200th anniversary of the passing of Wilberforce's bill, there is a growing awareness of just how much the world was developed by the slaves of Africa. And their songs and music, created by many unknown and forgotten musicians and writers, have inspired us in the past and will continue to do so in the future. The fact that these songs are still sung today is a testimony to their great struggle for justice and freedom, a heritage that has shaped world history.

PART ONE

RESISTANCE

1

The Boy Who Could Never Forget

It was his first memory, a moment of searing intensity that he carried all the days of his life.

He couldn't move. It felt as though his feet were stuck to the ground.

The memory was like a hot, burning coal scorching his bare skin. Every time it came to his mind, he trembled.

The boy would never forget the day his father's ear was cut off.

Josiah Henson was born a slave, like his parents, and was about five years old when he saw his father's head bloodied, his back raw and bleeding. Years later, he recalled, 'Father appeared one day covered in blood and in a state of great excitement . . . he was beside himself with mingled rage and suffering.'

Josiah's father had committed a heinous offence. He had struck a white man.

The incident had occurred when the slaves were at work in the fields. One of the overseers had attempted to rape Josiah's mother. Hearing her cries of anguish, his father rushed to the spot and stopped the assault. He would have killed the man if Josiah's mother hadn't pleaded for his life.

Josiah's father knew what to expect for striking a white man – whatever the reason. Slaves had been castrated or lynched for less.

He knew he had only one choice: run.

But where could he go? As a slave on his master's estate, he barely knew the territory, having perhaps a sketchy grasp of the plantation; beyond that was the mysterious unknown. He might have picked up specks of detail of the surrounding area from wagon drivers and house slaves who had accompanied their master into town, but Charles County in Maryland would have been mostly completely new to him.

Who could he turn to for help? Certainly, no white man. Any African like him would sympathize but most likely be powerless to respond. Where would he find slaves who had become freed men?

How would the master act when he heard the news of his escape from his hired hands? Advertise in the newspaper? What reward would he put up for his capture? Would he call in the bounty-hunters and slave-catchers? Get the bloodhounds to take up the scent and hunt him down? The dogs probably knew the layout of the land better than he did. How far could he get? And what would become of his woman, the mother of his young child, Josiah?

✦
Who could he turn to for help? Certainly, no white man
✦

His body was weak, every movement was a burden. For a short spell, Josiah's father hid out in the woods, scavenging for food, but hunger and despair found him. Desolate and alone, he turned, took the first few faltering steps and limped back to the plantation, a broken man.

Young Josiah may have been pleased to learn that his father had returned but unprepared for the trauma that was to follow. What happened next was forever etched into his mind. Later, he recalled:

> The day for the execution of the penalty was appointed. The Negroes from the neighbouring plantations were summoned to witness the scene. A powerful blacksmith named Hewed laid on the stripes. Fifty were given, during which the cries of my father might be heard a mile away and then a pause ensued. True, he had struck a white man, but as valuable property he must not be damaged. Judicious men felt his pulse. Oh! He could stand the whole. Again and again the thong fell on his lacerated back. His cries grew fainter and fainter, till a feeble groan was the only response to the final blows. His head was then thrust against the post and his right ear fastened to it with a tack; a swift pass of a knife and the bleeding member was left sticking to the place.

Josiah's father never recovered. He had been a jovial person who entertained people with his songs. The slaves from Africa had recreated an early version of the banjo and his father could be heard playing the instrument late in the evening or on their day of rest. 'But from this hour he became utterly changed. Sullen, morose and dogged,' Josiah wrote. 'Nothing could be done with him. No fear or threats of being sold to the far south – the greatest of all terrors to the Maryland slave – would render him tractable.'

All Josiah could recall was that his father was sent to Alabama. No one heard from him again.

Josiah's mother was the property of Dr Josiah McPherson who hired her out to Francis Newman, the owner of a farm near Chesapeake Bay. Josiah's father had been owned by Newman. Like other slave couples, Josiah's parents' marriage was a private arrangement with no legal protection. Slaves were sold at auction without consideration for family ties: husband to wife, mother to child, sister to brother. Slave preachers had adapted the marriage vows to read, 'till death or distance parts us'.

Josiah's mother and her young family of six children lived on Dr McPherson's estate. Slave families were usually crammed into tiny rooms, slept on bare floorboards and worked from dawn to dusk. Although life was bleak, there was one calamity that they feared particularly: the auction block.

> ✢
> **Slave families were usually crammed into tiny rooms, slept on bare floorboards and worked from dawn to dusk**
> ✢

When Dr McPherson died, his estate, including the slaves, were put up for sale, with the profits to be divided amongst his heirs. Josiah lamented, 'We were property – not a mother and the children God had given her.'

For Josiah, it was evident that the selling of people in this way could never be understood until it was experienced. He wrote:

> The first sad announcement that the sale is to be; the knowledge that all ties of the past are to be sundered; the frantic terror at the idea of being 'sent south'; the almost certainty that one member of the family will be torn from another; the anxious scanning of purchasers' faces; the agony at parting, often forever, with husband, wife, child – these must be seen and felt to be fully understood. Young as I was, the iron entered into my soul.
>
> The remembrance of the breaking up of McPherson's estate is photographed in its minutest features in my mind. The crowd collected around the stand, the

huddling group of Negroes, the examination of muscle, teeth, the exhibition of agility, the look of the auctioneer, the agony of my mother . . . I can shut my eyes and see them all.

My brothers and sisters were bid off first and one by one, while my mother, paralysed by grief, held me by the hand. Her turn came and she was bought by Isaac Riley, of Montgomery County. Then I was offered to the assembled purchasers. My mother, half distracted by the thought of parting forever from all her children, pushed through the crowd, while the bidding for me was going on, to the spot where Riley was standing. She fell at his feet and clung to his knees, entreating him in tones that a mother only could command, to buy her baby as well as herself and spare to her one, at least, of her little ones. Will it, can it be believed that this man, thus appealed to, was capable not merely of turning a deaf ear to her supplication, but of disengaging himself from her with such violent blows and kicks, as to reduce her to the necessity of creeping out of his reach and mingling the groan of bodily suffering with the sob of a breaking heart? As she crawled away from this brutal man, I heard her sob out, 'Oh, Lord Jesus, how long, how long shall I suffer this way?' I must have been then between five and six years old.[4]

Josiah was purchased by Isaac Riley's neighbour but when the child fell ill, Riley took on the boy but promised to pay only if he survived. 'A dead nigger' was no good to him, he grumbled. He was sold three times before he reached the age of eighteen.

One Sunday, Josiah was given permission to attend a church meeting. This was to be the turning point in his life as he was transformed by the message he heard. For the rest of his days, he would look back to it as 'an awakening to a new life'. He wanted nothing more than to tell others about his new-found faith.

He was owned by Amos Riley in Kentucky and one night Josiah accompanied his master when he went to the tavern to gamble. Riley was drunk and got into a fight with Bryce Litton. Josiah rescued his master, but Litton was determined to seek revenge and, with several of his slaves, grabbed Josiah. Josiah was held down and beaten with a fence rail until his shoulder blades shattered. Though he eventually healed, he could no longer raise his arm above his head. While working for Riley in Kentucky, Josiah was befriended by a Methodist preacher who devised a way for the youth to buy his own freedom. A price of $450 had been fixed but when Josiah returned with the funds, his master tricked him out of $350 and told him the price had increased to $1,000. He was still enslaved. Josiah wrote, 'I consoled myself as well as I could . . . resolved to trust in God and never despair.'

Married with four children, Josiah discovered that he was on the brink of being sold in New Orleans. But at the last moment, his master, Amos Riley Jr, fell ill and relied on Josiah to carry him back to Kentucky. Josiah decided to escape and after finally convincing his wife, the Henson family made their bid for freedom.

It was a perilous journey. They followed the North Star and after making it to the riverside, a fellow slave rowed them across the Ohio River; a native American tribe helped them survive the Ohio wilderness; the captain of a freight steamer ferried them from Sandusky to Canada; and finally, on 28 October 1830, they landed on free soil. Almost immediately, Josiah found work as a day labourer.

Josiah vowed to help other slaves and returned to Maryland and Kentucky on secret missions. Over time, he rescued hundreds of slaves, bringing them back to Ontario. There Josiah bought land and set up a school for former slaves. Nineteen years later, in 1849, he published his memoirs to raise money for the community. The autobiography[5] of his enslavement and escape inspired Harriet Beecher Stowe's best-selling novel *Uncle Tom's Cabin*. Her book created a sensation and, backed up by Josiah's authentic and haunting narrative, it stirred people to demand an end to slavery, leading directly to the Civil War.

In Canada, the fugitive slave became an active Methodist preacher and travelled to Europe. In London, the Archbishop of Canterbury asked him which college he had graduated from. Josiah replied, 'The College of Adversity.'

He was the first black person to be featured on a Canadian stamp, in 1983, the centennial of his death. The log cabin in which Josiah and other slaves were housed in

✦
In Canada, the fugitive
slave became an
active Methodist
preacher and travelled
to Europe
✦

Montgomery County, Maryland, is currently attached to a modern three-bedroom home at 11420 Old Georgetown Road, amidst a residential development in North Bethesda. The property and an acre of land were purchased with the intention of opening the cabin to the public.

Josiah Henson was one among many slaves who escaped to freedom but returned to rescue others.

Just one of the heroes of the Underground Railroad.

2

Slaves in the Land of the Free

By the time Josiah Henson was born, in 1789, slavery was an established institution in the Americas.

The Dutch brought the first African slaves to America in 1619 and sold them as indentured servants. The following year, English settlers arrived in the *Mayflower* and eventually plantations were set up but their experiment of using European labourers failed. Like everyone who needed a large labour force for the new burgeoning industries, they followed the example of Spain and Portugal and turned to Africa.

The total population of Africa in 1500 was thought to be about 47 million. Over the next 350 years, about ten to fifteen million Africans are estimated to have been stolen from the continent. About six million or more are believed to have died during their capture or on the crossing known as the Middle Passage. The countries involved in the slave trade included Portugal, Spain, France, Holland, Britain, Denmark and others. The slaves were taken to Brazil, the Spanish empire including Cuba, the British, Dutch and French West Indies and Europe; about five hundred thousand were sold in North America.

The slaves were bought mainly from the west coast of Africa – from territories now defined as the countries of

Senegal, Guinea, Gambia, Ghana, Sierra Leone, Liberia, the Ivory Coast, Togo, Benin, Nigeria, Cameroon, Gabon and part of the Congo republics. Explorers to the region discovered a sophisticated system of organisations with kings, governors and noblemen heading clans, tribes or similar kinship groups. Thus, the people groups separated into historical lineage traced to such tribes as the Fon, Yorubam Ibo, Fanti, Fulani, Ashanti, Wolof and Baoule.

In America, plantation crops such as cotton and tobacco, followed by sugar cane, indigo and rice, galvanized the demand for slave labour. The invention of the cotton gin in 1800 fuelled a greater need for a slave labour force and with the increase of the slave population, the institution of slavery was legalized.

By 1662, the children of all slave women were declared slaves in perpetuity. The rape of a female slave was not considered a crime unless it involved trespassing on another's property. Slaves were forbidden education and by 1669 a master could legitimately kill his slave while inflicting punishment. In 1818, Georgia set the huge sum of $1,000 as a fine for anyone who freed a slave. The state of Virginia declared that any freed black man who remained in the state for over a month became enslaved again automatically.

> ✦
> By 1662, the children of all slave women were declared slaves in perpetuity
> ✦

In 1857, a sensational legal case resulted in the extraordinary decision that African-Americans could not be citizens of the United States. Dred Scott was born a slave but had travelled and lived in the free states of Illinois and Wisconsin with his owner, and settled and married Harriet Robinson, a slave owned by a local justice of the peace. After the death of his owner, Scott sued for freedom but the Supreme Court eventually ruled in 1857 that anyone descended from slaves had no rights as a citizen. Chief Justice Roger Taney stated that because Scott was black, he was not a citizen and therefore had no right to sue. This decision became the most famous ruling of all slavery cases confirming to some that the US Constitution was a slave-owner's document.

The Christian Church initially did not oppose the practice of slavery; for fifty years the Anglican Church in Virginia debated whether to educate slaves amidst resistance from slave-owners who were convinced that their 'property' would revolt if taught the fundamentals of Christian beliefs. Slave-owners convinced themselves and others that blacks were inferior to whites and deserved to be enslaved. Individual Christians were certain the practice was wrong while the Quakers were the first group to condemn slavery. In 1775 they organized the first abolition society in the United States. Women were at the forefront in raising money for the cause, and funds were used to help slaves escape. Leaflets spread the word as petitions were sent to Congress. A 'Free Produce' campaign spread, intended to boycott Southern products, urging consumers to refuse to buy anything made or grown by slave labour.

In *Time Magazine*, Orlando Patterson observed:

> So emerged one of the great contradictions in the growth of American democracy. The region with the most vibrant democracy and the largest electorate was deeply committed to large-scale slavery and the strong conviction that there was no inconsistency between liberty and slavery. For black Americans, the consequences were tragic and lasting.[6]

Africans were viewed as possessions not people, treated as inferior outsiders, continually reminded that they did not belong and were permanently excluded from all basic rights of citizenship.

America emerged as a democracy entrenched in slavery. Many of the founding fathers, including Benjamin Franklin, George Washington and Thomas Jefferson, held human beings as property.

It seemed probable that Thomas Jefferson had children with one of his slaves, a girl named Sally Hemings, whose mother was owned by John Wayles, also rumoured to be her father. Wayles was Jefferson's father-in-law. Christopher Hitchens, Jefferson's biographer, observed that he 'opposed slavery on principle, but could never find the right political occasion to put his principle into practice. He was able to make progress against the trade in slaves, but not against the institution of slavery on American soil.'[7]

Jefferson thought slaves should be freed but they should be deported and not be allowed to stay on American soil. In Virginia, an African was considered a slave and laws were passed requiring freed blacks to leave the colony.

> ✦
> **Africans were viewed as possessions not people, treated as inferior outsiders**
> ✦

Plantation Life

In *Atlas of Slavery*, James Walvin noted, 'By the mid-century (1860), there were almost four million slaves, though only about 60 per cent worked in cotton. The USA no longer needed to import slaves from Africa, the slave states relying instead on an internal slave trade.'[8]

Walvin stated that there were about four hundred thousand slave-owners, though most of them owned only a handful of slaves.

Most workers were divided into two main categories: field hands and house servants. Everyone was expected to work in the fields: men, women and children.

In his autobiography, Josiah Henson recorded details of plantation life. As a child, he would carry buckets of water for the men at work in the field and hold the horse-plough that was used for weeding between the rows of corn. As he grew older, his chores increased; as a youth, a hoe was thrust into his hand and he took his place amongst the men and women in the fields.

Work started at dawn and finished at dusk. The labour force was fed twice a day, mostly cornmeal and salted herrings and buttermilk in summer.

The slaves were kept in log cabins, basic structures built on the bare earth; a few huts had wooden floors. About ten or twelve people; men, women and children, were crammed into each room and beds were improvised with straw and old rags, a single blanket their only covering. Josiah noted, 'Our favourite way of sleeping was on a plank, our heads raised on an old jacket and our feet roasting before the smouldering fire.'

In his compelling autobiography, Frederick Douglass, a towering figure in African-American history, recorded a gripping account of plantation life. He wrote:

> There were no beds given the slaves, unless one coarse blanket be considered such and none but the men and women had these . . . They find less difficulty from the want of beds, than from the want of time to sleep; for when their day's work in the field is done, the most of them having their washing, mending and cooking to do and having few or none of the ordinary facilities for

doing either of these, very many of their sleeping hours are consumed in preparing for the field the coming day; and when this is done, old and young, male and female, married and single, drop down side by side, on one common bed – the cold, damp floor – each covering himself or herself with their miserable blankets; and here they sleep till they are summoned to the field by the driver's horn.[9]

Violence was routinely used to motivate the enslaved to work, to establish discipline and to maintain order. Mutilations, brandings, whippings, hand and foot stocks and solitary confinement were common. Rape was widespread and family members were routinely separated and sold at auctions.

For Sale

Jacob Stroyer was one of fifteen children born on a plantation in South Carolina. He published *My Life in the South*[10] the story of his life during slavery, in which he described the experience of being sold:

✦
Violence was routinely used to motivate the enslaved to work
✦

> When the day came for them to leave, some, who seemed to have been willing to go at first, refused and were handcuffed together and guarded on their way to the cars by white men. The women and children were driven to the depot in crowds, like so many cattle and the sight of them caused great excitement among master's Negroes. Imagine a mass of uneducated people shedding tears and yelling at the tops of their voices in anguish and grief.

The victims were to take the cars from a station called Clarkson turnout, which was about four miles from master's place. The excitement was so great that the overseer and driver could not control the relatives and friends of those that were going away, as a large crowd of both old and young went down to the depot to see them off. Louisiana was considered by the slaves as a place of slaughter, so those who were going did not expect to see their friends again. While passing along, many of the Negroes left their masters' fields and joined us as we marched to the cars; some were yelling and wringing their hands, while others were singing little hymns that they were accustomed to for the consolation of those that were going away, such as:

When we all meet in heaven,
There is no parting there;
When we all meet in heaven,
There is parting no more.

We arrived at the depot and had to wait for the cars to bring the others from the Sumterville Jail, but they soon came in sight and when the noise of the cars died away we heard wailing and shrieks from those in the cars. While some were weeping, others were fiddling, picking banjo and dancing as they used to do in their cabins on the plantations. Those who were so merry had very bad masters and even though they stood a chance of being sold to one as bad or even worse, yet they were glad to be rid of the one they knew.

While the cars were at the depot, a large crowd of white people gathered and were laughing and talking about the prospect of Negro traffic; but when the cars began to start and the conductor cried out, 'all who are going on this train must get on board without delay', the colored people cried out with one voice as though the heavens and earth were coming together and it was so pitiful, that those hard hearted white men who had been accustomed to driving slaves all their lives, shed tears like children. As the cars moved away we heard the weeping and wailing from the slaves as far as human voice could be heard; and from that time to the present I have neither seen nor heard from my two sisters, nor any of those who left Clarkson depot on that memorable day.

After he was freed, in 1864, Stroyer became a minister of the African Methodist Episcopal Church.

In Raymond Bial's book *The Underground Railroad*[11] he quoted the slave, John Brown, recalling such auctions:

Here may be seen husbands separated from their wives, only by the width of the room and children from their parents, one or both, witnessing the driving of the bargain that is to tear them asunder forever, yet not a word or lamentation or anguish must escape from them; nor when the deed is consummated, dare they bid one another good-bye, or take one last embrace. Even the poor, dear, little children, who are crying and wringing their hands after 'daddy and mammy' are not allowed to exchange with them a parting caress. Nature, however, will not be thus controlled and in spite of the terrors of the paddle and the cowhide, the most fearful scenes of anguish and confusion take place.

Brown also described his own parting:

✦
At last we got to the gate and I turned around to see whether or not I could not get a chance of kissing my mother
✦

At last we got to the gate and I turned around to see whether or not I could not get a chance of kissing my mother. She saw me and made a dart forward to meet me, but Finney (the slave-trader) gave me a hard push, which sent me spinning through the gate. He then slammed it to and shut it in my mother's face. That was the last time I ever saw her, nor do I know whether she is alive or dead at this hour.

Brown eventually escaped and sailed to England in 1850 where he worked as a carpenter in London. In 1855, he dictated his story, *Slave Life in Georgia*.[12]

Original Documents: Letters About the Sale of Slaves

These two letters were addressed to Rice Carter Ballard, a slave-trader and planter, who purchased and managed plantations in Mississippi, Louisiana and Arkansas. He co-owned some of these slaves with Judge Samuel Boyd.

This first letter is from J.M. Duffield to Colonel Ballard who wants to buy a slave girl named Maria. From the evidence in the earlier part of the letter, it looks as though Duffield may have fathered a child with Maria:

From Jackson ('Private and in Confidence')

I desired, in the first place, to apprise you, that I had made arrangements to send the child northward, there to be brought up and educated and there forever to reside. I have made all my arrangements for her and she will start on the 6th July. I shall be in Natchez, when she goes . . .

The next was, to endeavour to do something for Maria. Her health seems to be sinking and she has been a sufferer of great agony mentally and bodily. You will recollect the cruelties which you described to me once in confidence that had been perpetrated, by a certain person in whose power Maria is [Judge Boyd] and I recollect the horror you expressed of it. All these cruelties have been inflicted upon the feeble frame of that girl – and are frequently inflicted – she must die under them. Long ago would I have freed her from them, if I had been able to do so . . .

Will you not, Colonel, let me have her. She is sickly, suffering and will die soon if she remains where she is. I buy her only to free her. Lashed as she is like an ox, until the blood gushes from her, I know, your kind, humane heart must revolt at the barbarities she is constantly enduring. I would do anything on earth to relieve her from her present position . . . Only listen to the dictates of your own kindly nature and you will grant the request, which I make as a matter of favor to me and goodness to her and as another memorial of your generosity.

The second letter is from a pregnant slave, Virginia Boyd, who asks Ballard to stop her from being sold:

Virginia Boyd to R.C. Ballard, 6 May 1853 – Houston, TX

To [Warrenton]

I am at present in the city [sic] of Houston in a Negro traders yard, for sale, by your orders.

I was present at the Post Office when Doctor Ewing took your letter out through mistake and read it aloud, not knowing I was the person the letter alluded to. I hope that if I have ever done or said anything that has offended you that you will forgive me, for I have suffered enough Cince [sic] in mind to repay all that I have ever done, to anyone, you wrote for them to sell me in thirty days, do you think after all that has transpired between me & the old man, (I don't call names) that its treating me well to send me off among strangers in my situation to be sold without even my having an opportunity of choosing for myself; its hard indeed and what is still harder for the father of my children to sell his own offspring. Yes his own flesh & blood. My God is it possible that any free born American would brand his character with such a stigma as that, but I hope before this he will relent & see his error for I still believe that he is possest of more honour than that. I know too that you have influence and can assist me in some measure from out of this dilemma and if you will God will be sure to reward you, you have a family of children & no [sic] how to sympathize with others in distress . . .

> ✦
> Its hard indeed and what is still harder for the father of my children to sell his own offspring
> ✦

Is it possible that such a change could ever come over the spirit of any living man as to sell his child that is his image. I don't wish to return to harass or protest his peace of mind & shall never try [to] get back if I am dealt with fairly . . .

I have written to the Old Man in such a way that the letter can't fail to fall in his hands and none others I use every precaution to prevent others from knowing or suspecting any thing I have my letters written & folded put into envelope & get it directed by those that don't know the Contents of it for I shall not seek ever to let any thing be exposed, unless I am forced from bad treatment &c

Virginia Boyd[13]

Slave Narratives

During the Depression of the 1930s, various government departments organized work projects to provide jobs for the unemployed. The United States Library of Congress set up a scheme for jobless writers to interview released slaves and this led to the publication of many slave narratives – over ten thousand pages of interviews with over two thousand former slaves. In *Before Freedom, When I Just Can Remember,*[14] Belinda Hurmence published excerpts from these historical documents of interviews with 284 former slaves from South Carolina. These are the raw, moving, authentic voices, told in their own words:

> **Jake McLeod, aged 83:** The overseer, he blow horn for us to go to work at sunrise. Give us task to do and if you didn't do it, they put the little thing on you. That was a leather lash or some kind of a whip. Didn't have no whipping post in our neighbourhood. They didn't have no jail in them days, but I recollect one woman hanged on the [gallows]. I ran away one time. Somehow the overseer know where I was. I recollects Old Missus had me tied to the tester bedstead and she whip me till the whup broke. I see her getting another arm about full and I tear loose and run away.

> **Elijah Green, aged 94:** Mr Ryan had a private jail on Queen Street near the Planters' Hotel. He was very cruel; he'd lick his slaves to death. Very seldom one of his slaves survive a whipping. He was the opposite to Governor Aiken, who live on the northwest corner of Elizabeth and Judith Streets. He had several rice plantations, hundreds of his slaves he didn't know.
>
> Not till John Calhoun's body was carried down Boundary Street was the name changed in his honour.

He is buried in St Philip's Churchyard, across the street, with a laurel tree planted at his head. Four men and me dig his grave and I cleared the spot where his monument now stand. The monument was put up by Pat Collington, a Charleston mason. I never did like Calhoun 'cause he hated the Negro. No man was ever hated as much as him by a group of people. On Charlmer [Chalmers] Street is the slave market from which slaves was taken to Vangue Range and auctioned off. At the foot of Lawrence Street, opposite Easy Bay Street, on the other side of the trolley tracks is where Mr Alonzo White kept and sell slaves from his kitchen. He was a slave-broker who had a house that extended almost to the train tracks, which is about three hundred yards going to the waterfront.

> ✦
> **On the other side of the trolley tracks is where Mr Alonzo White kept and sell slaves from his kitchen**
> ✦

One song I used to sing to the slaves when master went away, but I wouldn't be so fool as to let him hear me. What I can remember of it is:

Master gone away
But darkies stay at home
The year of jubilee is come
And Freedom will begun

Slaves was always buried in the night, as no one could stop to do it in the day. Old boards was used to make the coffin that was blackened with shoe polish.

Fannie Griffin, aged 94: My master, Master Joe Beard, was a good man, but he wasn't one of the richest men. He only had six slaves, three men and three women. But he had a big plantation and would borrow slaves from his brother-in-law, on the adjoining plantation, to help with the crops. I was the youngest slave, so Missy Grace, that's Master Joe's wife, keep me in the house most of the time, to cook and keep the house cleaned up. I milked the cow and worked in the garden too.

My master was good to all the slaves, but Missy Grace was mean to us. She whip us a heap of times when we ain't done nothing bad to be whipped for. When she go to whip me, she tie my wrists together with a rope and put that rope through a big staple in the ceiling and draw me up off the floor and give me a hundred lashes. I think about my old mammy heap of times now and how I'd seen her whipped, with the blood dripping off of her.

All that us slaves know how to do was to work hard. We never learn to read and write. Nor we never had no church to go to, only sometimes, the white folks let us go to their church, but we never join in the singing. We just set and listen to them preach and pray.

We ain't had no celebration after we was freed. We ain't know we was free till a good while after. We ain't know till General Wheeler come through and tell us. After that, the master and missus let us all the slaves go 'cepting me; they keep me to work in the house and the garden.

Prince Smith, aged 100: Some of the slaves had to work on Sunday to finish their week's work. If they didn't, the driver, who was a Negro, would give a lashing varying from fifteen to twenty-five chops. Only high-class masters had Negro drivers; the crackers had white overseers. Master had three kinds of punishments for those who disobeyed him. One was the sweat box. That was made the height of the person and no larger. Just large enough so the person didn't have to be squeezed in. The box is nailed and in summer is put in the hot sun; in winter it is put in the coldest, dampest place. The next is the stock. Wood is nailed on or with the person lying on his back with hands and feet tied with a heavy weight on his chest. The third is the bilbao [or bilbo: foot shackles]. You are place on a high scaffold for so many hours and you don't try to keep a level head, you'll fall and you will surely hurt yourself, if your neck isn't broken. Most of the time they were put there so they could break their necks.

Isiah Jefferies, aged 86: In warm weather we had cotton clothes and in cold weather we had woollen clothes that our master had made for us by the old ladies on the plantation. But we did go barefooted all winter until we was grown and married.

When I got to be a big boy, my ma got religion at the camp meeting at El-Bethel. She shouted and sung for three days, going all over the plantation and the neighbouring ones, inviting her friends to come to see her baptized and shouting and praying for them. She went around to all the people that she had done wrong and begged their forgiveness. She sent for them that had wronged her and told that she was born again and a new woman and that she would forgive them. She wanted everybody that was not saved to go up with her. The white folks was baptized in the pool first and then their darkies. When the darkies' time come, they sung and shouted so loud that the patrollers come from somewhere, but Master and Missus made them go away and let us shout and rejoice to the

> ✦
> **When I got to be a big boy, my ma got religion at the camp meeting at El-Bethel**
> ✦

fullest. Missus had all her darkies that was a-going in for baptizing to wear white calico robes made for everybody. My ma took me with her to see her baptized and I was so happy that I sung and shouted with her. All the niggers joined in singing. The white folks stayed and saw us baptize our folks and they liked our singing.

Robert Toatley, aged 82: Never had any money, didn't know what it was. Mammy was a housewoman and I got just what the white chillun got to eat, only a little bit later, in the kitchen. There was fifty or sixty other little niggers on the place. Want to know how they was fed? Well, it was like this: You've seen pig troughs, side by side, in a big lot? After all the grown niggers eat and get out the way, scraps and everything eatable was put in them troughs. Sometimes buttermilk poured on the mess, sometimes potlicker. Then the cook blowed a cow horn. Quick as lightning a passel of fifty or sixty little niggers run out of the plum bushes, from under the sheds and houses and from everywhere. Each one take his place and souse his hands in the mixture and eat just like you see pigs shoving around slops troughs.

My white folks, the Mobleys, made us work on Sunday time, with the fodder and when the plowing get behind. They mighty neighbourly to rich neighbours but didn't have much time for poor buckra.

Can read, but can't write. Our slaves was told if ever they learned to write, they'd lose the hand or arm they wrote with.

Sylvie Cannon, aged 85: I don't know exactly how old I is 'cause the peoples used to wouldn't tell they chillun how old they was before they was grown. There been about fourteen head of we chillun and they all gone but me. I the last one. Yes, ma'am. I been a little girl in slavery time. I just can remember when I was sold. Me and Becky and George. Just can remember that, but I know who bought me. First belong to the old Bill George and that where Miss Earlie Hetchel bought me from. Never did know where Becky and George went.

I see 'em sell plenty coloured peoples away in them days, 'cause that the way white folks made heap of they money. Course, they ain't never tell us how much they sell 'em for. Just stand 'em up on a block about three feet high and a speculator bid 'em off just like they was horses. Them what was bid off didn't never say nothing either. Don't know who bought my brothers, George and Earl.

I see 'em sell some slaves twice before I was sold and I see the slaves when they be travelling like hogs to Darlington. Some of them be women folks looking like they going to get down, they so heavy.

Yes, ma'am, the Bill Greggs had a heap of slaves 'cause they had my grandmammy and my granddaddy and they had a heap of chillun. My mammy, she belong to the Greggs, too. She been Mr Greggy's cook . . . I remembers she didn't talk much to we chillun. Mostly, she did sing about all the time:

Oh Heaven, sweet Heaven
When shall I see?
If you get there before me
You tell my Lord I on the way

Oh, that be a old song what my grandmammy used to sing way back there.

The white folks didn't never help none of we black people to read and write no time. They learn the yellow chillun, but if they catch we black chillun with a book, they nearly 'bout kill us.

Savilla Burrell, aged 83: My master in slavery time was Captain Tom Still. He had big plantation down there on Jackson Creek. My missus's name was Mary Ann, though she wasn't his first wife. My pappy name Sam; my mother name Mary. My pappy did not live on the same place as Mother. He was a slave of the Hamiltons and he got a pass sometimes to come and be with her, not often. Us lived in a log cabin with a stick chimney. The

> ✦
> My pappy did not live on the same place as Mother
> ✦

bed was nailed to the side of the walls. Just one room. Never seen any money. Us half naked all the time. Grown boys went around barefooted and in their shirt tail all the summer.

Old Master was the daddy of some mulatto chillun. The relations with the mothers of those chillun is what give so much grief to Missus. The neighbours would talk about it and he would sell all them chillun away from they mothers to a trader. My missus would cry about that. They sell one of Mother's chillun once and when she take on and cry about it, Master say, 'Stop that sniffing there if you don't want to get a whipping.' She grieve and cry at night about it.

Young Master Sam Still got killed in the Civil War. Old Master live on. I went to see him in his last days and I sat by him and kept the flies off while there. I see the lines of sorrow had plowed on that old face and I remembered he'd been a captain on horseback in that war. It came into my remembrance the song of Moses: 'The Lord has triumphed glorily and the horse and his rider have been throwed into the sea.'

Profits

The racism that emerged directly from slavery and the concepts that upheld the institution of slavery weren't imported by the Europeans who arrived in America. These ideas grew on American soil.

Many of the immigrants had left behind deprivation and discrimination and found themselves part of a privileged category. No matter how poor or degraded they were, the poor whites were considered superior to Native Americans and Africans. As a result, the institution of slavery was able to flourish. Through intimidation, changing laws and mob violence, these new citizens achieved superiority and denied others their citizenship. Under Andrew Jackson's rule, working class people gained rights many had not known before, including the right to vote.

✦
One was his newly-discovered 'Drapetomania', a disease which caused slaves to run away
✦

The people who benefited from the system were white men. Native Americans, Africans and women were not included.

Negro Diseases

Dr Samuel Cartwright, a highly respected and widely published medical specialist from the University of Louisiana, wrote authoritatively in 1851 on two diseases, which he asserted were unique to African-Americans. One was his newly-discovered 'Drapetomania', a disease which caused slaves to run away; the other, 'Dysaethesia Aethiopica', caused 'rascality' in black people, both freed and enslaved.

Dr Cartwright's advice for preventing and curing such diseases was that slaves struck down with 'drapetomania' should be kept in a submissive state and whipped if they deteriorated to the point of actually attempting to run away. He assured slave owners that 'rascality' could also be cured by whipping.

He confidently declared, 'With the advantages of proper medical advice, strictly followed, this troublesome practice that many Negroes have of running away can be almost entirely prevented, although the slaves be located on the borders of a free state, within a stone's throw of the abolitionists.'

James Henry Hammond, a senator and wealthy plantation owner from South Carolina, was an outspoken defender of slavery. In 1893, he bought a female slave with a young daughter; the woman became his mistress and he fathered several children with her and later replaced her, as his mistress, with her own twelve-year-old daughter.

Hammond developed an idea called the 'mudsill' after observing that a mudsill is the lowest threshold that supported the foundation of a building. He outlined his 'Mudsill theories' to the US Senate on 4 March 1858 and declared, 'In all societies there must be a class to do the menial duties, to perform the drudgery of life.' Hammond argued that there must and always had been, a lower class for the upper classes to rely on.

Resistance

History has been described as documenting events over time. Those who decide the events to be recorded – and remembered – control history. How we view slavery in the United Kingdom has largely been defined by those commenting on the slave trade and controlling how we recall the era of slavery – and so we remember William Wilberforce but we don't remember Olaudah Equiano.

Much has been recorded about the abolitionists and those who fought to end the slave trade, but the resistance of the slaves themselves has been obscured. In fact, the slaves of Africa resisted at the first – and every – opportunity. Revolts and rebellions arose all through the era of slavery – despite brutal reprisals.

More than five hundred cases were documented of uprisings on sea and land showing that such events were closely monitored.

The largest slave revolt prior to the American Revolution occurred in 1739 near Charleston, South Carolina, with twenty-four whites killed and at least forty-four blacks executed. In retaliation, it became a crime to teach a slave to read and write while the playing of drums was banned.

Gabriel Prosser, a slave blacksmith, tried to seize Richmond, Virginia, in 1800 with an army of about a thousand slaves. They killed all whites except Quakers, Methodists and Frenchmen, and could have succeeded if a massive rainstorm hadn't flooded roads and washed out bridges. Prosser and twenty-six of his followers were hanged.

In 1822, Denmark Vesey tried to burn down Charleston, at the time the sixth largest city in the United States, and aimed to start a revolution against slavery. Vesey was betrayed by an informer and he was caught and hanged with thirty-four collaborators. Vesey had earlier won $600 in a street lottery in 1800 and purchased his freedom.

Nat Turner led the most famous slave revolt in American history in 1831. Convinced that he had a divine mission to lead a violent revolution, he directed seventy followers in the nation's bloodiest slave uprising ever seen. Turner's followers went from plantation to plantation and massacred everyone they encountered. The murder count reached sixty before he was caught and publicly executed.

Fugitive slaves who made it to Spanish Florida were protected by Native Americans and came to be known as 'Seminoles' after the Creek word for 'runaway'. The Spanish governor set up Fort Mose, made up almost exclusively of slaves; it was the first known freed black community in North America. Soldiers from the community fought alongside Native Americans in order to retain their Florida homelands.

Maroon (meaning 'fugitive' or 'runaway') or fugitive communities became notorious for their effective guerrilla warfare and rebel forces waged successful, though sometimes short-lived, campaigns against the colonial forces.

The idea of individual rights and independence sparked revolutions in France and America, yet such champions of liberty found no irony in their practice of slavery. With Christians fuelling a demand for the rights of all people to be respected, such concepts inspired a freedom movement in Saint-Dominique (Haiti) and in 1791 slaves started to fight against the island's plantation owners and the French army, and did so for the next two years, creating the first black republic. It was the first successful slave rebellion in the Americas and the Haitian revolution haunted every slave society until slavery was abolished. It also motivated slaves in other territories to fight for their freedom.

✦
The idea of individual rights and independence sparked revolutions in France and America
✦

Three generations of John Brown's family were white abolitionists and, as a child, he had seen a young slave boy beaten with a shovel. This experience became the defining moment in his life. In 1798, his father, Owen Brown, took part in the forcible rescue of some slaves claimed by a Virginia clergyman in Connecticut. John Brown grew to be a passionate abolitionist who believed that God had chosen him to lead the battle against slavery and this led him to take up a wild and dangerous plan. He intended to set up a stronghold in the Virginian mountainside, from where he intended to use commando-styled tactics to raid the surrounding plantations and rescue slaves who would then be whisked away to Canada, using routes and hiding places suggested by people like Harriet Tubman. He was convinced that this strategy would spark similar uprisings across the country.

Brown's first step was to attack the federal arsenal at Harpers Ferry, Virginia, but the US military overpowered the group and he was tried for murder, slave insurrection and treason, and convicted and hanged in 1859. Reverend S. Peet met Brown on the day he set off for Harpers Ferry and tried to stop him warning that he could lose his life. Brown told the clergyman, 'I believe I have been raised up to work for the liberation of the slave; while the cause will be best advanced by my life, I shall be preserved; but when that cause will be best served by my death, I shall be removed.'

On the day of his execution, he handed one of his guards a paper on which he had written, 'I am quite certain that the crimes of this guilty land will never be washed away except with blood.'

John Brown marched to Harpers Ferry with twenty-one men, sixteen of whom were white, including three of his sons, and five blacks. The group included Barclay and Edwin Coppock, young brothers from a devout

Quaker farmer. Barclay escaped but Edwin faced the death penalty. From his prison cell he wrote to a relative:

Charleston, 13 December 1859

Joshua Coppock:

My Dear Uncle – I seat myself by the stand to write for the first and last time to thee and thy dear family. Though far from home and overtaken by misfortune, I have not forgotten you. Your generous hospitality towards me, during my short stay with you last spring, is stamped indelibly upon my heart and also the generosity bestowed upon my brother who now wanders, an outcast from his native land. But thank God, he is free. I am thankful it is I who has to suffer instead of him.

The time may come when he will remember me. And the time may come when he may still further remember the cause in which I die. Thank God the principles of the cause in which we were engaged will not die with me and my brave comrades. They will spread wider and wider and gather strength with each hour that passes. The voice of truth will echo through our land, bringing conviction to the erring and adding members to the glorious army who will follow its banner. The cause of everlasting truth and justice will go on

✦

Our beloved country is the land of the free and the home of the brave; but that cannot be

✦

conquering and to conquer until our broad and beautiful land shall rest beneath the banner of freedom. I had fondly hoped to live to see the principles of the Declaration of Independence fully realized. I had hoped to see the dark stain of slavery blotted from our land and the libel of our boasted freedom erased, when we can say in truth that our beloved country is the land of the free and the home of the brave; but that cannot be.

I have heard my sentence passed; my doom is sealed. But two more short days remains for me to fulfil my earthly destiny. But two brief days between me and eternity. At the expiration of those two days I shall stand upon the scaffold to take my last look of earthly scenes. But that scaffold has but little dread for me, for I honestly believe I am innocent of any crime justifying such punishment. But by the taking of my life and the lives of my comrades, Virginia is but hastening on that glorious day, when the slave will rejoice in his freedom and say, 'I, too, am a man and am groaning no more under the yoke of oppression.'

But I must now close. Accept this short scrawl as a remembrance of me. Give my love to all the family. Kiss little Joey for me. Remember me to all my relatives and friends.

And now farewell for the last time.

From thy nephew,

Edwin Coppock[15]

Two days after writing this letter, Edwin Coppock walked to the gallows and was hung by the neck until dead in the slave state of Virginia.

The celebrated French writer Victor Hugo, in exile in Guernsey, tried to seek a pardon for Brown but failed. Hugo warned of a possible civil war breaking out.

John Brown became a symbol of a nation coming apart at the seams and his words proved prophetic. Within one year, the Civil War had begun.

Running Away Was a Sign of Protest

Like Josiah Henson's father and, sometime later, Josiah himself, many thousands of slaves followed the same compelling instinct: to run.

They ran away in groups and formed maroon communities. They ran away in couples or families. Some ran alone. Fugitives lived in swamps and mountain ranges to elude capture. Some took off for Florida and Mexico. Most tried to head North.

The Mason–Dixon Line was the boundary separating Pennsylvania from Maryland – the free North from the slave South. Anyone who reached the line and could cross it knew they had found sanctuary, albeit temporary and uncertain.

Slaves who crossed the line were disappointed with life in the North. No longer enslaved, they were not considered equal. And they still lived in constant danger.

The American Constitution stated in 1787 that any slave who escaped to a free state had to be returned to their owner. The first Fugitive Slave Act, in 1793, made it a crime to help a runaway slave or to stop a fugitive's arrest. Later, a more severe law was passed which made it easier for slave-catchers to capture both runaways and freed Africans who had crossed the Mason–Dixon Line and were living in the North.

✦
Slaves who crossed
the line were
disappointed with life
in the North
✦

In 1850, the issues of slavery and land threatened to split the Union. Washington, the nation's capital, permitted slavery and had housed the largest slave market in North America, but a political battle erupted every time a new state joined the union: should slavery be allowed?

After the gold rush of 1849, California had developed and progressed and wanted to enter the Union as a free state. Could this be permitted? When a large territory was won after victory with Mexico the same question rattled the corridors of power: what about slavery?

After a thundering debate over whether slavery would be allowed in Texas, California, Utah and New Mexico, the Southern states threatened to break away and form their own country. The deadlock was broken by Henry Clay, a Kentucky senator, who negotiated a deal known as the Compromise of 1850. This included the controversial second Fugitive Slave Act.

This law made it illegal for anyone to help an escaped slave and enabled Southern slave-owners to reach into any territory and reclaim their runaway 'property'. The fugitive had no right to a trial or to appeal against their capture. Commissioners would deal with cases and be paid $5 if the prisoner won his release, $10 if their owner claimed them. The process of registering a claim for a runaway was changed making it easier for slave-owners. Furthermore, any US Marshall who refused to return a runaway slave would pay a fine of $1,000. The states of Virginia and North Carolina treated slave helpers the same as horse thieves – both offences carried the death penalty.

The second Fugitive Slave Act threatened respected black citizens who had settled in free Northern states. It meant they could be seized from their homes and returned in chains to the plantations. It made the abolitionists even more determined and Underground Railroad activity increased. The Act also made slavery a national issue.

While some historians suggested that the influence of the Fugitive Slave Act has been exaggerated, Raymond

Bial, author of *The Underground Railroad*, explained, 'The passage of the Fugitive Slave Law and the alarm of the slave-holders are clear indications that the railroad not only threatened but damaged the institution of slavery.'[16]

For slaves, getting off the plantation or farm was difficult and making plans to escape was a risky business. A whisper overheard by the wrong people would wreck everything and place everyone in trouble. Those captured, or their collaborators, faced a whipping, the isolation pen, or worse.

✦

For slaves, getting off the plantation or farm was difficult and making plans to escape was a risky business

✦

Just knowing where to run was valuable knowledge. Which direction headed North? The best clue was to identify the North Star. Unlike any other stars, it never changed its position and pointed in only one direction: North.

The North Star had been used by explorers and adventurers to trace their journey and for slaves in the South this became their fundamental focus of direction. Josiah Henson, Harriet Tubman and James Pennington, among others, followed the North Star to lead them to freedom.

To locate the North Star, they turned to a collection of stars with a formation that looked like a 'dipper' – a cup with a long handle. Two stars on the cup's edge always pointed to the North Star. This group of stars came to be known as the Drinking Gourd, a hollowed out gourd to dip and drink water. By identifying the 'drinking gourd' in the sky, night travellers could always locate and follow, the North Star.

While planning their escape, it became important to find new ways to communicate. Keeping secrets became the key to success. Everyday things such as songs held hidden messages and 'Wade in the Water' and 'Follow the Drinking Gourd' became known as coded songs, even though the exact original words and details of such songs were unlikely to have been preserved

Slaves and conductors used quilts to send coded messages. It was common for quilts to be hung out to dry like washing on a line; such messages could be displayed in plain sight, without arousing the suspicion of slave-owners. Quilt patterns carried messages and codes. A monkey-wrench pattern could mean it was time to collect the tools needed for an escape. Geometric patterns, ties, knots, stitches and colour choices functioned together as a means of conveying messages, according to *Hidden in Plain View*.[17] Some quilt patterns carried a map of a plantation and surrounding territory: important geographical information that most slaves would be unaware of.

To the owner and others on the plantation, such things may have seemed puzzling or innocuous but to slaves on the run, they meant the difference between life and death.

3

Runaway Train

The Underground Railroad was not underground and it was a not a railroad.

It was simply the most dramatic protest action against slavery in the history of the United States. A secret operation that employed cloak and dagger tactics with highly ingenuous but dangerous devices. People risked their lives and property to rescue slaves and helped them reach freedom, demonstrating sacrifice and heroism on an epic and unprecedented scale.

Although the railway was used, slaves escaped using any means possible. Charles Blockson, a historian of the movement, explained that the Underground Railroad 'was a network of paths through the woods and fields, river crossings, boats and ships, trains and wagons, all haunted by the spectre of recapture.'[18] This loosely constructed network of routes started in the South, worked its way through the North and ended in Canada. Others escaped to Florida, Mexico or overseas.

Despite the risks, slaves were determined to escape

✦
Although the railway
was used, slaves
escaped using any
means possible
✦

and in the North, there were people, both black and white, ready to help.

John Fairfield, a white abolitionist and the son of a slave-holding family, posed as a slave-trader to rescue Africans. In Cincinnati, he disguised twenty-eight fugitives in a funeral procession; even a hearse was hired to complete the illusion. Fairfield watched with a twinkle in his eye as unsuspecting slave-hunters removed their hats in respect as the fugitives marched slowly past.

Allen Pinkerton used his cooper's barrel-making and crafts shop near Chicago as an underground depot. Later, the Scottish-born lawman went on to start the first detective agency, as he hunted down members of the Jesse James gang, the Reno Brothers and Butch Cassidy. He gained legendary status through many Hollywood movies.

In another town, a telegram operator learned of an impending raid on a safe house where fugitives were hiding. The operator passed on the information and the slaves were moved.

The complaints stacked up and bounty-hunters and slave-catchers were constantly on the prowl.

Slaves on the run had been given food and temporary shelter at a tavern in Bloomfield, Ohio. After they set off, slave-hunters arrived and the pub keeper told them they were nearby and could easily be caught. He convinced the posse to spend the night in his tavern. The next morning he organized a series of misadventures that kept the group at the tavern: he failed to wake them and let them sleep in; the key to the stables went missing; each horse had a shoe missing; blacksmiths prolonged the process to re-shoe the horses. By the time the bounty-hunters finally got going, the band of fugitives had reached another hide-out.

The first documented reference that slaves received help while fleeing was made by George Washington in a letter in 1786. He whinged that one of his runaway slaves was helped by a 'group of Quakers, formed for such purposes'.

Origin of the Name

When the first steam locomotives and steel rails of the 1800s arrived, their popularity gave the rescue operation its name. There are several versions of how the term originated and came to be linked with the rescue operation.

Tice Davids was on the run after escaping in Kentucky in 1831. His owner was hot on his trail and was closing in when the runaway slave reached the Ohio River. With no time to think, the fugitive plunged into the water and swam to the opposite shore. The slave-owner grabbed a boat and chased him in close pursuit and saw Davids scramble up the bank and vanish from view. The master reached the riverbank and searched everywhere but Davids was nowhere to be found. No one in the nearby city of Ripley could recall seeing Davids and eventually the slave-owner returned to Kentucky completely baffled. He told friends that his slave must have disappeared on an 'underground railroad'.

According to *Passages to Freedom*, sympathetic residents of the city sheltered Davids and quickly moved the runaway to safety. Ripley was home to the Reverend John Rankin, an ardent abolitionist who aided refugees like Davids for forty years. Slave-owners offered rewards as high as $2,500 for the 'abduction or assassination' of Rankin. Rankin's house has been preserved and today the building is a US national historic landmark.

Passages to Freedom reported that slave-hunters in Pennsylvania made a similar comment after a similarly frustrating escapade when slaves they were pursuing eluded them. Yet another account places the origin of the name to an incident in Washington in 1839; after a fugitive slave was tortured he admitted that he was to have been sent North, where 'the railroad ran underground all the way to Boston'.[19] In *The Underground Railroad*, Raymond Bial noted that seventeen runaways were hidden in Levi Cotton's house in Newport (later Fountain City) Indiana. Bial wrote, 'Frustrated slave-hunters complained, "There's an underground railroad around here and Levi Cotton is its president!"'[20]

The Underground Railroad called on the language of rail journeys. 'Stations' were run by 'stationmasters' and the routes from each safe house were called 'lines'. People who helped were known as 'agents'. Runaways were known as 'packages' or 'freight'. Anyone who contributed money or goods became 'stockholders'. Lanterns lit by oil were hung on poles outside homes signifying that fugitives would be welcomed.

+

The Underground Railroad called on the language of rail journeys

+

Stopping places and safe houses were referred to as 'stations' and 'depots'. Some of these locations had hidden rooms, fake walls, false bookshelves, sliding panels, hiding places with secret passages, concealed tunnels, basements that could be reached only through a concealed trap door, or holes dug in the shafts of wells. Edward Morris's Bull's Tavern in Pennsdale, Pennsylvania had secret panels at the top of each staircase. The Lewelling Quaker House in Salem, Iowa is now a museum with its covert spaces on view.

Elizabeth Barnett Piatt, the wife of Judge Benjamin Piatt, was an agent and a statue on their lawn held a code. If the decorative figure held a flag, runaways were welcome; if the flag was missing, the judge was at home and fugitives should pass on. Handshakes, passwords and coded knocks were used to alert stationmasters that fugitives were nearby and needed sanctuary.

Cities such as Rochester, conveniently located near Canada, played an important role with many stations, stationmasters and stockholders. Some of the homes used as stations still exist today. Former slave Frederick Douglass used his own home as one of the stations and numerous sites in the area were used as safe houses.

Those who risked their lives to help fugitive slaves were called 'conductors'. Sometimes a conductor posing as a slave would covertly enter a plantation and guide the runaways out of the area, moving at night and hiding out in barns and other remote locations.

When a conductor was in the area, the spirituals sung at slave gatherings took on new meaning. Although the words of the original songs

✦

A song such as 'Swing Low, Sweet Chariot' would most likely have been sung as a code

✦

may be lost to history, the music that has been preserved and passed along provides clues. 'Steal Away to Jesus' would have had a meaning beyond devotion.

A song such as 'Swing Low, Sweet Chariot' would most likely have been sung as a code, as the line 'chariot [or conductor] coming for to carry me home' would alert the slave (who had planned to escape) that it was time to move. The lyrics of this classic spiritual are as follows:

Chorus:
Swing low, sweet chariot
Coming for to carry me home
Swing low, sweet chariot
Coming for to carry me home.

I looked over Jordan and what did I see
Coming for to carry me home
A band of angels coming after me
Coming for to carry me home.

(Chorus)

Sometimes I'm up and sometimes I'm down
Coming for to carry me home
But still my soul feels heavenly bound
Coming for to carry me home.

(Chorus)

The brightest day that I can say
Coming for to carry me home
When Jesus washed my sins away,
Coming for to carry me home.

(Chorus)

If I get there before you do
Coming for to carry me home
I'll cut a hole and pull you through
Coming for to carry me home.

(Chorus)

If you get there before I do
Coming for to carry me home

Tell all my friends I'm coming too
Coming for to carry me home.

(Chorus)

The Underground Railroad had to operate in secrecy
and many details have gone unrecorded or are difficult
to verify beyond the stories passed down through the
oral family tradition. Still, it captured public imagination as a symbol of freedom and reached its peak
between 1810 and 1850. Though statistics vary, about
thirty thousand to one hundred thousand people travelled this route to reach freedom.

Slave-owners placed 'Wanted' posters in newspapers
promising rewards for the capture of runaways. Under the
Fugitive Slave Laws, when runaways were caught, they
had no right to a jury trial and
could not testify in their
defence. Federal marshals or
bounty-hunters could swear
an oath promising to return
the 'property' to the owner,
and frequently freed slaves
were captured and resold.

⚹

Load of potatoes,
parcel or freight =
fugitives expect
fugitives

⚹

Slaves were sometimes disappointed on reaching
their destination, facing racism and discrimination, and
states such as Indiana prohibited blacks from settling in
the area.

These phrases were part of the Underground Railroad
Code:

The wind blows from the south today = a warning
  that there were bounty-hunters around
A friend of a friend = a password signalling the arrival
  of fugitives

The friend of a friend sent me = a password used by
fugitives travelling alone

Load of potatoes, parcel or freight = fugitives expect
fugitives

A friend with friends = railroad conductors signalled
to the listener that they were a conductor

William Still documented accounts of fugitives and
recorded communication; he confirmed that messages
were encoded and understood only by those involved in
the Underground. For example, 'I have sent via at two
o'clock four large and two small hams', meant that four
adults and two children were sent by train from
Harrisburg to Philadelphia. The word 'via' indicated
that they were not on the regular train but travelling by
another route or station.[23]

4

The Great Escape

The Underground Railroad is an epic story of courage and collaboration and ordinary people made it happen. What they accomplished, individually and together, changed the course of history.

Josiah Henson

After his escape, Josiah Henson settled with his family in Canada and became a prominent church leader. One Sunday morning, he preached a fiery sermon about Christian responsibility towards those in bondage in the South. After the service, James Lightfoot, a refugee who, like Henson, had escaped from Kentucky, told the preacher that he was stirred by the sermon and felt compelled to act. Lightfoot asked Henson if he could rescue his family who were still enslaved and, after plans were finalized, Henson made the perilous journey into the slave country of the Southern states. Covertly, he made contact with Lightfoot's parents but they were deemed too elderly to survive the journey North and the other relatives were reluctant to leave without their elders. Unprepared for such a tumultuous decision, Lightfoot's family asked if the 'conductor' could return a year later for them.

While down South, Henson heard of slaves on a near-by plantation who were ready to escape, so he secretly made contact and guided them to safety. He knew that he faced arrest if caught but he made the treacherous journey one year later and returned for Lightwood's relatives. Henson followed the North Star to navigate his passage and used stations of the Underground Railroad network as they fled.

Harriet Tubman

Harriet Tubman was born a slave in Maryland's Dorchester County around 1820 and was hired out as a house servant when she was about six years old. Harriet's task was to stay awake all night and ensure that the family's baby wouldn't wake the mother. If Harriet fell asleep, the baby's mother whipped her.

> ✦
> If Harriet fell asleep,
> the baby's mother
> whipped her
> ✦

A wiry, feisty, rebellious child, she described here the first time she ran away

I was only seven years old when I was sent away to take car' of a baby. One mornin' after breakfast I stood by de table waitin' till I was to take it; just by me was a bowl of lumps of white sugar . . . I never had nothing good . . . an' dat sugar . . . did look so nice, an' my Missus's back was turned to me so I jes' put my fingers in de sugar bowl to take one lump, an' she turned an' saw me. De nex' minute she had de raw hide down; I give one jump out of de do', an' I saw dey came after me, but I jes' flew

and dey didn't catch me. I run, an' I run, an' I run. By an'
by, when I was clar tuckered out, I come to a great big
pig-pen . . . I stayed from Friday till de nex' Chuesday,
fightin' wid dose little pigs for de potato peelin's an'
oder scraps . . . By Chuesday I was so starved I knowed
I'd got to go back to my Missus, I hadn't got no whar else
to go.[22]

When she returned, Harriet was beaten but it didn't stop
her trying again. Knowing that she could be whipped at
any point, she often put on thicker clothing to ease the
pain.

Harriet was ten when she saw an overseer recognize
a runaway slave. In fury, the man threw a two pound
lead weight at the fugitive, but he ducked and the object
hit the child, its full force knocking her unconscious. She
wasn't deemed worthy of medical attention but was
allowed a day and a half's rest and was then back in the
fields, blood streaming down her face. She never fully
recovered and was plagued throughout her life with
seizures that may have been a form of epilepsy.

A few years after she married, aged about twenty-
two, Harriet discovered that she was to be sold and tried
to escape. She followed the North Star but this attempt
failed; undeterred, she tried again, some months later.
Helped by several 'stations' along the way, she eventually reached Pennsylvania and recalled later, 'There was
such a glory over everything; the sun came like gold
through the trees and over the fields and I felt like I was
in heaven. I had crossed the line.'

Freedom infused Harriet with a determination to
bring her family out of bondage. She took any job available and worked regularly in kitchens, saving every
penny to fund her journey South, one year later. If
caught, she faced certain arrest but fearless and spirited,

she stepped into the danger zone, time and again. Moving stealthily, she escorted her sister and her two children to safety. Bolstered by this success, she worked, saved more money and returned for a series of tenacious rescue missions that took on legendary status and earned her the nickname 'Moses'.

Nothing could deter her from her central purpose and she pursued this mission with fierce determination. Empowered by a fervent faith, she was convinced that she was God's chosen agent and pursued her compelling new purpose in life with devoted zeal.

✦

Freedom infused Harriet with a determination to bring her family out of bondage

✦

She once came face to face with her own former master on a street in Cambridge. With quick thinking and spontaneous action, she created a distraction and quietly slipped away in the confusion.

She loved to sing and composed songs herself. On the night before she ran away for the first time, she walked past the slave dwellings singing loudly. At one point, she saw her owner but, to disarm him, she sang even louder. She told later how the master looked back at her puzzled. He had good reason to be suspicious; she was gone by the morning. Her song said:

> I'm sorry, I'm going to lebe you/Farewell, oh farewell
> But I'll meet you in the morning/Farewell oh farewell
> I'll meet you in the mornin'/I'm boun' for de promised land
> On the oder side of Jordan/Bound for the promised land
> I'll meet you in the mornin'/Safe in de promised land

On the other side of Jordan/Bound for de promised
  land

She was known to hide her band of weary pilgrims out
of sight while scouting out the territory ahead. If all was
well, she would sing out a hymn of praise and the fugitives would break cover. If danger lurked, she would
sing out a warning, something like:

Go down Moses
Way down in Egypt's land.

In Troy, New York, a crowd gathered after Charles Nalle,
a runaway slave who had been captured under the Slave
Fugitive Act, was detained at the office of the United
States Commissioner. With brazen tenacity, Harriet disguised herself as a frail elderly pensioner, draped in a
shawl and clutching a food basket. The guards gave her
a cursory glance and waved her through to the second
floor where the outlaw was held under guard.

No one could have predicted the chaos and whirl-
wind created by such an innocuous figure as Tubman as
she single-handedly launched a commando-style raid to
free the prisoner. One eye witness reported 'She was
repeatedly beaten over the head with policemen's clubs,
but she never for a moment released her hold . . . until
they were literally worn out with their exertions and
Nalle was separated from them.'[23]

The battle raged between the abolitionists led by
Tubman who wrenched the captive from federal marshals and spirited him away. It was an audacious and
bold operation that boosted her reputation.

The *Troy Times* covered the story: 'The rescuers numbered many of our most respectable citizens, lawyers,
editors, public men and private individuals. The rank

and file, though, were black and African fury is entitled to claim the greatest share in the rescue.'

By 1856, Tubman's notoriety led to a $40,000 reward for her capture – dead or alive. She once passed some men in front of a 'Wanted' poster for herself and heard them remark that the criminal slave rescuer was illiterate. Instinctively, she pulled out a book and pretended to read. The moment passed without incident.

✦

Tubman couldn't read but had a commanding knowledge of the Bible

✦

Tubman couldn't read but had a commanding knowledge of the Bible. She told an agent of the Underground that she knew no fear because she 'ventured only where God sent'.

Frederick Douglass

Frederick Douglass was a passenger on the Underground Railroad and became one of its most famous 'stationmasters' in Rochester, New York. He was a gifted speaker and charismatic intellectual whose towering presence made him the most influential African-American of his time.

He was born Frederick Bailey on a farm on Maryland's eastern shore. As an infant, his mother was hired out to work on a plantation about twelve miles away. It was general practice at the time to separate slave children from their mothers. Years later he wrote, 'I do not recollect of ever seeing my mother by the light of day. She was with me in the night. She would lie down with me and get me to sleep, but long before I waked she was gone.'

His mother, Harriet Bailey, walked the journey of several miles after toiling all day in the fields, spent a few hours with her child and then retraced her steps back to start work again at dawn the next day. As a field hand, she would be whipped if she wasn't at her place at sunrise.

He'd heard rumours that his real father was the plantation owner, Aaron Anthony, but it made little difference to the way he was treated. Raised by his grandmother till he was about six years old, he was removed and lived rough, recalling that he ate cornmeal mush from a trough 'like so many pigs'.

Three years later, Frederick was on the move again. He was sent to Baltimore, aged about nine years old, to work for Hugh Auld, the manager of a shipbuilding firm. Here he did odd jobs and looked after Mr Auld's young son, whose mother was influenced by Frederick's enthusiasm and charm. She taught him the alphabet and a few words but this good will gesture came to an abrupt halt when Auld reminded his wife that it was against the law for slaves to be educated.

Frederick grasped that literacy was the key to freedom. He used every opportunity to develop his skills, sometimes enticing white children to teach him to read in exchange for whatever money he'd been able to save.

His next master, Edward Covey, was proud of his capability as a 'slave breaker'. Covey thrashed his young slave repeatedly until one day he resisted. The risk was great and Frederick could have been killed for retaliating, but Covey most likely didn't want to have his reputation damaged by admitting that he was beaten by a youth he couldn't control.

It was a turning point in Frederick's life. His physical conquest over Covey was diminished in comparison to the victory over his own internal fear. 'I felt as I never felt before . . . My long crushed spirit rose, cowardice departed, bold defiance took its place; and I now resolved that, however long I might remain a slave in form, the day had passed forever when I could be slave in fact.'

Four years later, he took the step into the cold, deep darkness of the unknown. The decision to escape was intense and overpowering, yet frightening. He'd heard that slaves were free men if they reached Canada. With a devout and abiding faith, he'd sung songs of praise with secret appeals of hope while living under the shadow of slavery that covered the land. Years later he spoke of a song called 'Run to Jesus, Shun the Danger, I Don't Expect to Stay Much Longer Here', with the comment that this was the first time that he'd considered the idea of escaping from slavery. In his own account, he wrote:

> We were at times remarkably buoyant, singing hymns and making joyous exclamations, almost as triumphant in their tone as if we had reached a land of freedom and safety. A keen observer might have detected in our repeated singing of 'O Sweet Canaan, sweet Canaan/I am bound for the land of Canaan' something more than a hope of reaching heaven. We meant to reach the North and the North was our Canaan.

✦
Like every other slave, he had never seen a map, had no concept of the terrain, or the distances between locations
✦

On the plantation grapevine, he'd picked up the significance of following the North Star. But stepping into the mysterious landscape held fears. Like every other slave, he had never seen a map, had no concept of the terrain, or the distances between locations. And everything beyond the plantation was like some hazy object far on the horizon. He recalled, 'The real distance was great enough, but the imagined distance was, to our ignorance, much greater.'

The dangers were like rain clouds overhead. He knew that just crossing the border and reaching the North didn't guarantee safety. Advertisements for runaway slaves filled the newspapers with 'Wanted' posters around town offering rewards for their capture. Bounty-hunters and slave-catchers would hunt him down. If caught, he would return in handcuffs and chains to an uncertain fate.

This psychological pressure intensified alongside the determination to escape. 'On the other hand,' he wrote, 'far away, back in the hazy distance where all forms seemed but shadows under the flickering light of the North Star, behind some craggy hill or snow-capped mountain, stood a doubtful freedom, half frozen and beckoning us to her icy domain.'

The scent of freedom was a powerful, driving force. His first attempt failed but two years later, he whispered his great secret to his common-law wife, Anna Murray, and decided to try again. Disguised as a sailor and carrying false papers, he boarded a train to Delaware, later a steamboat for Philadelphia and another train bound for New York. The journey that had started years ago as a secret in his heart had taken 24 hours to complete.

New York was a lonely, dangerous city for a man on the run. He kept to the shadows and moved with stealth, ever alert for gunmen and traitors who would turn him in. He found temporary shelter in the home of David Ruggles, a black activist, who realized he could be jailed for hiding a fugitive. Meanwhile, Ruggles arranged for Anna Murray to escape; even though they were 'hopeless, houseless and helpless', their love overshadowed every problem and Frederick and Anna were married in his home by a slave preacher, James Pennington, of whom more later.

Douglass emerged as a new generation of abolitionist. His first hand experience of being enslaved, combined with his remarkable intellect, placed him as a formidable presence in the battle against slavery.

He saw through hypocrisy and exploitation, rejecting both. At first, he was paraded amongst Northern audiences and encouraged to stutter, act dazed and roll his eyes in a parody of a 'thing' or 'chattel'. He also noted that white agents of the organisation received over twice the salary of their slave speakers. A devout Christian, he was disappointed that churches would only offer the sacraments to Christian slaves after the white congregation had been served. Recalling the hypocrisy of slave-owners, Douglass recognized a difference between 'the Christianity of this land and the Christianity of Christ . . . to receive one as good, pure and holy, is of necessity to reject the other as bad, corrupt and wicked'.

He developed a strong Christian leadership in an all-black congregation and was a gifted orator and authoritative intellectual who wanted to contribute to the anti-slavery movement. Apparently, he often started his meetings with these words, 'I appear before you as a thief and robber. I stole this head, these limbs, this body from my master and ran away from him.'

He published the *North Star*, a popular newspaper, from the basement of the African Methodist Episcopal Zion Church in Rochester and championed women's rights, speaking at the first women's rights convention in 1848. The sheer sight of women attending anti-slavery rallies outraged the nation. At the time, a delegation of American women activists travelled to London to attend the World Anti-Slavery Convention, held in London in 1840, but the British movement forbade women from attending as delegates, confirming that women were 'constitutionally unfit for public or business meetings'.

Douglass refused to ride in segregated train compartments reserved for blacks and was usually forcibly evicted from those reserved for whites. His fame made him an easy target and he was frequently attacked. Once when visiting Levi Cotton, a prominent abolitionist, he was mobbed, hit with a club that broke his hand and still assaulted while lying on the ground. Local Quakers helped Douglass escape but when a member of the mob was arrested, two hundred local pro-slavery supporters marched on the jail and won his release.

✦

Douglass refused to ride in segregated train compartments reserved for blacks and was usually forcibly evicted from those reserved for whites

✦

Douglass had once been a passenger on the Underground Railroad but he soon became a 'station-master' providing safety for fugitives and runaways.

His book, *A Narrative of the Life of Frederick Douglass, An American Slave*, was a best-seller and brought him even more acclaim but placed him at risk, exposing his status as a runaway slave.[24] He travelled to England where two admirers raised money so that he could buy his freedom. Douglass returned to America as the most influential African-American of his time but more importantly – as a freed man.

David Ruggles

David Ruggles, as we have seen, was the first to help the fugitive Frederick Douglass when he arrived in New

York City and understood the risks of aiding a runaway slave. Ruggles, an activist, was one of the first to refuse to sit in the 'coloured only' sections of railway cars and steamboats and was routinely ejected from the white-only areas. In 1841, he filed a series of anti-discrimination law-suits and invited both black and white abolitionists to join him in acts of civil disobedience.

James Pennington

James Pennington, the pastor who performed Frederick Douglass's wedding ceremony, was born Jim Pembroke. He described his life in slavery in this way: 'It is quite easy to imagine, then, what was the state of my mind, having been reared in total moral midnight.'

Some slaves were sold, others were hired out to local farm owners, but Jim Pembroke, along with his mother and older brother, were given as a wedding gift to a son of his master, a wheat farmer. Pembroke worked as a blacksmith and stonemason and took pride in his achievement as a skilled craftsman and considered him-self a valued part of planta-tion life. Somehow, he man-aged to allow the enduring degradation of slave life to pass by unnoticed. The turning point came one day when his owner caned him brutally. Pembroke's offence was simply looking his mas-ter directly in the face, eye-ball to eyeball. This humiliation was the turning point in his life and Pembroke reached a decision about his future. He decided to run.

> Jim Pembroke, along with his mother and older brother, were given as a wedding gift to a son of his master

The first day was frightening; he felt 'chilled to the heart'. His second night was spent huddled under a bridge. By the third night, he discovered that he had been heading in the wrong direction. Desolate and hungry, he stumbled across a white youth who immediately recognized Pembroke as a runaway slave. The young man warned him that there were slave patrols on the prowl and directed him to a house where someone would help him.

Still weary and dazed, he couldn't recall the words of the boy and within a short distance discovered it was too late. The patrols had caught sight of him and within minutes he was brought down, handcuffed and dragged to a local tavern where he was named as the 'runaway nigger'. The posse's first question was: what was the reward for his capture?

Puzzlingly, the posse took off and placed him under the watch of a young boy whom he was able to elude. When the alarm was sounded, Pembroke could hear the thunder of the horses but somehow managed to stay one step ahead of the hunters. At one point, the horsemen were close and he could hear them talking about the chase and their quarry. The noises of the night were deceptive. The clamour from the horses reverberated in the darkness of the night, the sounds echoing around him, as a storm broke overhead. Even the earth seemed to tremble under his feet from the thunder of the horses' hoof beats. At times, it felt as though his chest would be crushed and his heart stop beating. Jim recalled, 'Every nerve in my system quivered, so that not a particle of my flesh was at rest.'

The runaway slave stumbled through the thicket of vines, thistles and brambles, amidst the tangle of the undergrowth. The driving rain gave him cover; it washed away his tracks and stopped the bloodhounds on his trail from picking up his scent. But it also hid the North Star, making it hard to follow a clear path ahead. Pembroke didn't think he'd ever get out alive, but after an exhausting ordeal, the sound of the horsemen grew dim. He slumped to the ground, exhausted but content in the realization that he'd evaded the posse of slave-hunters.

The rest of the journey was made at night, following the North Star; with little food, he eventually crossed the line and stumbled into Pennsylvania, a weary and bedraggled figure, where the leader of the Underground Railroad in the area, William Wright, gave him lodging for six months. During this period, he learned to read, avidly studied the Scriptures and settled in New York, where he took the name Pennington. His curiosity increased and the knowledge that there were thousands of slaves in captivity troubled him deeply. Later, he wrote, 'I was in an agony. I thought I would make it a subject of prayer to God, although prayer had not been my habit, having never attempted it but once.' He prayed and fasted over the next three weeks haunted by the question, 'What shall I do for the slave?'

Stirred and challenged, Pennington felt compelled to serve in some way. In response, he trained for the ministry and played a prominent role in the African community, offering solace and spiritual counsel. He was active in the abolitionist circles and became a 'stationmaster' in the Underground Railroad.

In 1839, he organized help for Joseph Cinque and the Africans who had been arrested as a result of the Amistad mutiny. Two years later he published *The Origin and History of the Coloured People* and later an autobiography, *The Fugitive Blacksmith*.[25] In 1843, Pennington was a representative at the World Anti-Slavery Convention in London.

Harriet Jacobs

Harriet Jacobs was a heroic figure in the mould of Anne Frank, demonstrating the same tenacity and courage that we associate with the Jewish girl who hid from the Nazis in a house in Amsterdam but was captured and eventually died of typhus in Bergen-Belsen's notorious concentration camp.

Born into slavery, Harriet considered that her childhood was happy. 'I was so fondly shielded that I never dreamed that I was a piece of merchandise.'

After her mother's death, she worked as a house servant for her mother's owner and taken into the master's home. But the apparently benevolent gesture had a hidden motive. Things turned sinister as the kindly arm around her turned out to belong to a sexual predator and the next few years were dominated by intrigue, turbulence and sexual obsession.

Harriet's owner, Dr James Norcom, developed an intense fixation and infatuation for the young Harriet, aged fifteen, and 'whispered foul words' into her ear.

The rape of a slave woman by her owner was not a crime and Dr Norcom was rumoured to have fathered several children by his slaves. He warned Harriet that he would kill her if she betrayed him, but somehow, she resisted his advances and eluded becoming his latest sexual conquest; revolted by his presence, she became involved with another white man, a lawyer, and bore him two children. Infuriated, Dr Norcom refused to sell her or her children to their natural father; instead, he made plans for them to work as plantation slaves. Amidst the raging internal turmoil of

✦
The rape of a slave woman by her owner was not a crime
✦

leaving her children, twenty-one-year-old Harriet took the painful decision to escape.

Dr Norcom advertised a $100 reward for her return and with 'Wanted' posters up all over town, he hunted her relentlessly.

Under such intensive pressure, it was considered unsafe for Harriet to flee the area. Instead, her grandmother and uncle built a secret passage for her above a porch in their house. The space was nine feet long and seven feet wide with a slanting ceiling of three feet. Inside the crawl space, with no light or ventilation, she was unable to turn without scraping her shoulder. Rats and mice crawled over her and rain soaked her bedding and clothes.

Dr Norcom eventually sold her children to the lawyer and for a time they lived in the same house where Harriet had hidden herself. At first, she lived in total darkness, but later drilled a small hole that let in a ray of light. She read the Bible and watched the world move around her, occasionally seeing Dr Norcom walk past. She sometimes even saw her children and watched them as though they lived on another planet.

Her faith was taken to the limit. She wrote, 'I asked why the curse of slavery was permitted to exist and why I had been so persecuted and wronged from youth upward. These things took the shape of mystery, which is to this day not so clear to my soul as I trust it will be hereafter.'

Incredibly, she survived seven years in the crawl space, emerging only at night to stretch and exercise.

In 1842, plans were finalized for her to escape by sea. The passage for this fugitive slave to travel to Philadelphia was the same cost as a voyage to England. She sneaked on board terrified that she would be betrayed or caught by a bounty-hunter, but ten days later the ship docked without incident. In Philadelphia she faced a new ordeal. Unprepared for life outside, in a bustling city where she was a stranger, Harriet's fear of capture intensified. Her first few steps in freedom were taken in fear and trepidation. The first person she talked to on the waterfront was a Christian minister, who visited the port regularly and was on the lookout for runaways.

Harriet's new friends in the Underground travelled with her to New York, where she settled near Frederick Douglass and worked in a room above the office of his newspaper, the *North Star*. In time, she published her own moving account of her life recounting slavery days. Her story was first published in the *New York Tribune* but her account of sexual abuse so shocked the general public

✦

Her first few steps in freedom were taken in fear and trepidation

✦

that she had difficulty getting her autobiography published. Others were upset by the inclusion of material that exposed the role of the church in maintaining the institution of slavery. It was not until 1861 that Harriet's book was published in Boston entitled *Incidents in the Life of a Slave Girl*.[26]

In time, she was also reunited with her son and daughter and with her brother, John. The lawyer who had fathered Harriet's children had been elected to Congress and took her brother John to Washington to work for him as his servant. One day, John just walked out. The note he left his owner read:

> Sir
> I have left you, not to return.
> When I have got settled, I will give you further satisfaction.
> No longer 'Yours'

Sexual Violence Against Girls and Women

Harriet's experiences were not unusual. African girls and women worked alongside the men in the fields. They felt the lash of the whip, were regularly raped and routinely faced sexual abuse from their slave-owners. Her autobiography was probably the first to reveal the extent of sexual exploitation that enslaved girls and women experienced.

In Missouri, sixty-year-old Robert Newsom bought a fourteen-year-old girl called Celia to be his sexual slave and for five years she endured his relentless molestations. Unable to take his assaults any longer, Celia struck and killed Newsom with a log, but when the case came to trial, the jury were instructed that they couldn't consider her motives or intentions. *Passage to Freedom* noted 'Even if Celia killed her owner in self-defence, the jury was to render a verdict of guilty.'[27] As in other counties at the time, an owner's assault on slave girls was considered trespass not rape; clearly, owners could not trespass on their own property.

Celia was tried and hanged.

Anthony Burns

Anthony Burns was owned by Charles Suttle of Alexandria, Virginia, who awarded his slave many privileges. Burns paid his master a fee and in exchange could hire himself out to others; he supervised the hiring of other slaves and took on additional jobs. Burns learned to read and write, joined

✦

He was stirred by the idea that 'Christ came to make us free'

✦

a church and became a preacher. He was stirred by the idea that 'Christ came to make us free', and in 1854 the slave preacher boarded a ship to Boston in pursuit of liberty. Once on free soil, Burns wrote a letter to his brother, also owned by Suttle, but the document fell into the slave-owner's hands. Suttle realized he had to move fast if he was to retrieve his valuable possession.

With the element of surprise and the law on his side, the slave-owner headed for Boston to claim his 'property'. The recent Fugitive Slave Act compelled law officers to return slaves to their owners and police arrested Burns on a trumped up charge and jailed him in a cell on the third floor of the federal courthouse.

Boston was a stronghold of abolitionists and two groups met separately; one black, one white, to discuss their response. Thomas Higginson, a white minister, led a group who charged the courthouse with a beam used as a battering ram. Higginson and others forced their way in but were beaten back by deputies. In the melee, a shot was fired and a deputy stabbed to death. Hundreds of supporters thronged the courthouse and it took a larger group of militia and marines to regain control and uphold the court's verdict to return Burns to his slave-owner.

On 2 June 1854, a federal ship docked and waited for its infamous prisoner. Police shackled Anthony Burns and, shielded by armed guards, he was escorted to the waterfront past an estimated crowd of fifty thousand people who had lined the streets to catch a glimpse of this notorious man.

A black church immediately organized a fund raising campaign and purchased Burns's freedom for $1,300 and, one year later, he was back in Boston. A free man.

At a black church service in New York in February 1855, Burns spoke about his capture. The text first appeared in the *New York Tribune* and was reprinted in the *Liberator*, 9 March 1855, the first abolitionist newspaper, started by William Garrison, who worked full time for the cause. Burns's message began:

> My friends, I am very glad to have it to say, have it to feel, that I am once more in the land of liberty; that I am with those who are my friends. Until my tenth year I did not care what became of me; but soon after I began to learn that there is a Christ who came to make us free; I began to hear about a North and to feel the necessity for freedom of soul and body. I heard of a North where men of my colour could live without any man daring to say to them, 'You are my property;' and I, determined by the blessing of God, one day to find my way there. My inclination grew on me and I found my way to Boston.
>
> You see, I didn't want to make myself known, so I didn't tell who I was; but as I came to work, I got employment and I worked hard; but I kept my own counsel and didn't tell anybody that I was a slave, but I strove for myself as I never had an opportunity to do before. When I was going home one night I heard some one running behind me; presently a hand was put on my shoulder and somebody said: 'Stop, stop; you are the fellow who broke into a silversmith's shop the other night.' I assured the man that it was a mistake, but almost before I could speak, I was lif-ted from off my feet by six or seven others and it was no use to resist. In the Court House I waited some time and as the silversmith did not come, I told them I wanted to go home for supper. A man then come to the door; he didn't open it like an honest man would, but kind of slowly opened it and looked in. He said, 'How do you do, Mr. Burns?' and I called him as we do in Virginia, 'Master!'
>
> He asked me if there would be any trouble in taking me back to Virginia and I was brought right to a stand and

didn't know what to say. He wanted to know if I remembered the money that he used to give me and I said, 'Yes, I do recollect that you used to give me twelve and a half cents at the end of every year I worked for you.' He went out and came back next morning. I got no supper nor sleep that night. The next morning they told me that my master said that he had the right to me and as I had called him 'Master', having the fear of God before my eyes, I could not go from it. Next morning I was taken down, with the bracelets on my wrists – not such as you wear, ladies, of gold and silver – but iron and steel, that wore into the bone.

After regaining his freedom, Burns attended Oberlin College in Ohio and eventually became a minister.

The Father of the Underground Railroad

Harriet Tubman risked capture by stepping into the dangerous South to rescue slaves. When she led her weary band of exhausted fugitives back to the North, she turned to a few trusted people for help. In Philadelphia, the first person she sought out was William Still, whose legendary work would prompt the *New York Times* to title him 'the Father of the Underground Railroad'.

Still, the youngest of eighteen children, was born free after his father, Levin, enslaved in Maryland, had purchased his freedom in 1807. Still worked for the Pennsylvania Anti-Slavery Society and turned both his home and office into the nerve centre for the local abolitionist movement. His office organized escapes, offered practical help and, at one point, assisted about sixty fugitives per month. He proved to be the Underground Railroad's most important historian, keeping meticulous records and interviewing runaways.

According to James Horton, Still's records contained, 'dates, names and details of fugitives and those who assisted them, as well as routes and locations of safe houses throughout the East [with] information on abolition agents and collaborators in the slave South'. The information was dangerous and would have put lives at risk if it had fallen into the wrong hands and Still guarded the documents with his life. Like a spy, he stepped cautiously down the street and when certain that he wasn't followed, made his way to an old cemetery on the outskirts of town. He stashed the secret papers in a building inside and didn't retrieve them till slavery had been abolished. Finally, in 1872, he published an extraordinary collection of stories and reports entitled *Underground Railroad.*[28]

Still's most unforgettable experience occurred when a runaway slave appeared at his office and asked for help in tracing the man's family after a separation of forty years. The man told Still that he had been 'stolen away' when he was six years old and had been sold numerous times since then. The slave offered sketchy details but Still was held spellbound by the story he heard. The stationmaster realized that he was face to face with his own brother. Still wrote, 'I shall not attempt to describe the feelings of my mother and the family on learning the fact that Peter was one of us; I will leave that for you to imagine.'

> ✦
>
> The man told Still that he had been 'stolen away' when he was six years old and had been sold numerous times since then
>
> ✦

When Philadelphia's first street cars opened for business, only whites were allowed to use them. All through the 1860s, African-Americans were banned from the seats but were sometimes allowed to perch on the top or travel outside the cars. Still campaigned for equality, petitioned the authorities, brought legal action against the company and lobbied the state legislature. In 1867, a law was passed ending discrimination in street cars.

Ellen and William Craft

William Still was the man every runaway slave wanted to meet in Philadelphia. Everyone knew that if they could reach him, they would find safety, practical assistance and a push towards the next step in their journey to freedom. Still knew the names and addresses of just about everyone who would help and could advise fugitives about the routes to take to avoid slave patrols.

Still was the first to welcome Ellen and William Craft and help them on their way to Boston. Their epic three-day journey by train and steamship from Georgia was one of the most daring escapes ever attempted.

The man, a Southern plantation owner, walks in front, his face covered with a linen bandage to ease the pain of a toothache, his arm in a sling. His slave walks subserviently behind, carrying the luggage and explains that his master cannot speak because of the pain in his jaw and cannot fill in the hotel register because of an injury to his wrist. Despite this, the master finds a few words to exchange with others regarding the trouble caused by runaways.

✦

Their epic three-day journey by train and steamship from Georgia was one of the most daring escapes ever attempted

✦

The odd couple's journey started in Georgia on the day after Christmas and covered first class travel by coach, train and steamship, ending three days later, when they landed in Boston. Only then could their extraordinary story be told.

The disguise fooled everyone and created a sensation in abolitionist circles when it was revealed that the couple were really runaway slaves: William and Ellen Craft. Ellen was light skinned and passed for a white plantation owner who couldn't speak because of a 'toothache' and couldn't write because 'his' arm was bandaged and in a sling – not because he/she had never been educated.

Their exploits hit the press and the reports were closely followed by their owner who hired two slave-catchers, Knight and Hughes, to claim his 'property'.

When the slave-hunters hit town, the local stationmaster, Lewis Hayden, himself a runaway slave, sprang into action. The Crafts were moved from house to house to avoid capture. Meanwhile the slave-hunters were hounded in the street and faced a barrage of lawsuits: for carrying concealed weapons; for smoking in the street; for swearing; for trying to kidnap the Crafts. Each lawsuit required substantial bail.

The slave-hunters were further embarrassed as they were unable to locate a legal officer in the city who would serve the Crafts with a warrant for their arrest.

Determined not to abandon their assignment, Knight and Hughes traced Hayden, the stationmaster, to his home, where they found him sheltering yet another fugitive. Surrounded by armed men, Hayden stood on his front porch and held a lighted torch in his hand. He warned the slave-catchers that the house was rigged with gunpowder: 'Take one step closer and I'll blow everyone up.'

Stung by such a response, Knight and Hughes backed down and left town.

Boston was clearly an abolitionist stronghold but Presidential threats to send in the military made it clear that the Crafts had run out of hiding places. Fearing imminent capture, they were legally married and money was raised to fund a passage for the couple on the next ship to England, where slavery had been abolished. The couple stayed in England and didn't return until after the American Civil War.

Henry 'Box' Brown

'It was a matter of secrecy and danger,' the stranger whispered to William Still.

Samuel Smith, a white shoemaker in Richmond, Virginia, had travelled to Philadelphia to discuss an electrifying plan with the legendary abolitionist and others who had gathered together to meet him.

Smith related the story of Henry Brown, a slave he knew, who sang in the Baptist Church in Richmond. After Brown's wife and children had been sold and shipped out, he decided to escape. Brown, a devout Christian, believed he received a message from God while praying. The slave explained, 'There darted into my mind these words, "Go, get a box and put yourself in it."'

The plan that he thought that God had given him was to ship himself in a box to be sent as a shipping crate from Richmond to Philadelphia by railroad, three hundred and fifty miles away.

Brown was convinced and he managed to persuade others, offering to pay $100 to anyone in Philadelphia who was willing to receive this human cargo.

As Smith explained the audacious plan to Still and others in Philadelphia, eyebrows were raised, jaws dropped open, questions cascaded down, but eventually a deal was set. No one accepted the money Brown offered but they supported a safe passage for the desperate enslaved man and Still agreed that their address could be used to receive the 'cargo'.

Smith returned to Richmond with the news that Brown's astounding plan had found sympathetic supporters.

Around 4 a.m. on 29 March 1849, Smith and a friend from the Baptist church met Brown with the specially constructed box, three foot long, two foot wide and two foot eight inches deep, lined with baize cloth. Brown climbed into the box and positioned himself carefully inside as water and biscuits were passed to him. Holes were drilled near his face for air and the lid was sealed. Inside the box, Brown couldn't move as the darkness engulfed him. The crate was carefully marked 'This side up. Handle with care.'

> ✦
> Inside the box, Brown couldn't move as the darkness engulfed him
> ✦

The consignment was registered with Adams Express to be delivered to the address of the anti-slavery office in Philadelphia, three hundred and fifty miles away. Smith had the package delivered to the railway express office where it was set on a wagon and driven to the station. At Potomac Creek, the baggage was offloaded and placed aboard a steamer.

Brown experienced small miracles along the way. The box was hurled aboard with little regard for the sign regarding its fragility or care and landed upside down; Brown found himself on his head for some of the journey.

At one point, he was in a 'dreadful position' and found he couldn't move his hand to his face. Inside the crate, it was stifling hot. In continued anguish and discomfort, Brown recalled, 'My eyes were almost swollen out of their sockets . . . a cold sweat covered me from head to foot . . . every moment I expected to feel the blood flowing over me, which had burst from my veins.'

He started to pray earnestly and soon afterwards, he heard a passenger complain that he had to stand. Someone threw Brown's box on the floor so that it landed evenly and the man sat on the crate with a fellow traveller.

At Washington, the box was removed, placed on a wagon and taken to the railway depot and awaited a connecting train to Philadelphia. Inside the crate, Brown listened with intense frustration as he heard the voices of railway workers explain that the wagon was full and his box would have to wait for the following day's luggage train. The next voice saved Brown's life as a railway clerk insisted that regulations must be obeyed. 'Boys, the crate came with the Express, it must travel with the Express. Find some space!' The package was loaded but again Brown's box landed upside down; it shifted later and he travelled upright for the remainder of the journey.

Twenty-seven hours later, the railway Express rolled into Philadelphia's station with the crate on board. To avoid suspicion, Still had arranged through an intermediary for the box to be delivered to his office and with trusted friends they surrounded the crate when it arrived. Still's friend, Mr McKim, tapped on the side of the box.

'All right?' Mr McKim called out.

The reply was instant, 'All right!'

The lid was removed and Brown stepped from the box 'as wet as if he had come up out of the Delaware

✦

His fame had made him an easy target and, to evade capture, he sailed for England

✦

River', Still reported. Brown extended his hand to the group, 'How do you do, gentlemen,' and then fainted.

After he revived, it was like 'a resurrection from the grave of slavery'. Brown told the group he had one promise to fulfil and spontaneously burst into a song of praise: 'I waited patiently for the Lord and He heard my prayer.'

Later, Brown wrote, he was surrounded by men 'bidding me a hearty welcome to the possession of my natural rights'.

Brown became a popular speaker in abolitionist circles but soon after the US Senate passed the second Slave Fugitive Act in 1850, he was attacked on the streets of Providence, Rhode Island, probably by slave-hunters. His fame had made him an easy target and, to evade capture, he sailed for England, delighting audiences with stories of his extraordinary escape.

Samuel Smith

Henry 'Box' Brown's helper, Samuel Smith, remained active in the Underground and helped at least two other slaves escape but both were captured. Smith was arrested for his part in these attempted 'crimes' and faced financial ruin after losing all his property. No witnesses were allowed to testify at his trial and he was imprisoned for eight years, held for five months chained in a cell four feet by eight feet. An assassin was bribed to kill him and he was stabbed five times in the chest – but survived. Despite sustained pressure, the Governor of the prison refused to pardon Smith. Finally, when he was released, Smith received a hero's welcome and his courage and commitment have not been forgotten.

Stationmasters of the Underground Railroad

While stationmasters usually kept their work hidden and secret, the **Reverend John Rankin** made public his mission to help runaways and challenged slave-owners to stop him. Rewards rose to $2,500 for his murder but he managed to elude his assassins. Reverend Rankin fervently preached that all men were created equal and that God had 'made of one blood all nations of men'.

Jonathan Walker was imprisoned for helping seven slaves from Florida and had the letters 'SS' for 'slave stealer' branded on his hand.

Thomas Garrett's home in Delaware became known as the last stop before the free state of Pennsylvania and about two thousand runaways passed through its open door. A $10,000 reward was offered for his capture and he was eventually arrested, charged and fined severely. Garrett, a staunch Quaker, said he was worried about losing what little he owned and said, 'but now that you have relieved me, I will go home and put another storey on my house, so that I can accommodate more of God's poor'.

Garrett auctioned his personal possessions to pay the fine of $5,400. When marshals and law officers warned him of future 'crimes', Garrett replied, 'I haven't a dollar in the world, but if thee knows a fugitive anywhere on the face of the earth who needs a breakfast, send him to me.'

Three years later, Garrett opened his front door to find Harriet Tubman with eleven runaways in need of shelter and, true to his word, he immediately welcomed them inside. Garrett gave all of the refugees new shoes and hid them in a secret room in his home till they could move on to the next stationmaster.

Alexander Ross

In *North Star to Freedom*, Gena Gorrell recorded the story of Alexander Ross, a doctor from Belleville, Ontario, who made regular 'bird-watching' trips to the Southern states.[29] He was welcomed by plantation owners who never suspected Ross's clandestine activity, but at night he would slip out and pass secret messages with directions to Canada, giving out knives, compasses and a little money to those slaves who intended to get away.

Ross helped a slave named Joe escape but was arrested for his 'crime'. He was about to be convicted – and severely punished – when Joe walked into the courtroom and explained that he hadn't run away but had merely gone on a trip to visit his brother. The runaway slave had heard about the doctor's arrest and had given up his freedom to save him. The story has a happy ending: Ross was dining at a Boston hotel two years later, when one of the waiters greeted him warmly. It was Joe. After the doctor was safe, Joe took off and this time his getaway was successful.

Levi Coffin

Levi Coffin was known as the 'President' of the Underground Railroad. He was seven when he saw a bedraggled group of slaves pass by, chained and handcuffed. He asked one of the men why they were chained.

The man replied, 'They have taken us away from our wives and children and they chain us lest we escape and go back to them.'

The child never forgot that compelling encounter. He was raised a Quaker and moved to Indiana where he and his wife ran a general store. Over the next twenty years, they became active station-masters and helped over two thousand fugitives pass through on their journey North. The Coffins used a wagon to transport slaves, hidden in a compartment covered by bags of grain. When they moved to Cincinnati, their home was turned into a refuge, once again, with fugitives hidden for weeks without visitors or guests who rented rooms there realizing that others were living in the house.

✦

They have taken us away from our wives and children and they chain us lest we escape and go back to them

✦

Bound for Canaan by journalist Fergus Bordewich reported that Levi and his cousin Vestal Coffin were the founders of the earliest known scheme to transport fugitives across hundreds of miles of unfriendly territory to safety in the free states.[30] Pro-slavery fanatics frequently threatened to hang Coffin and to burn down his home.

Coffin is thought to have rescued and helped about two thousand slaves. When someone asked the devout Quaker why he helped slaves, Coffin replied, 'The Bible, in bidding us to feed the hungry and clothe the naked, said nothing about color and I should try to follow out the teachings of that good book.' Another time he commented wryly, 'I thought it was always safe to do right.'

In 1875, Levi Coffin published *Reminiscences*, an enthralling account of his experiences and some of the rescue operations that he had undertaken.[31] This is the story of a girl called Jane:

Jane was a handsome slave girl, who lived in Covington, Kentucky, her old master and mistress having moved from Virginia and settled in that place some years before the time our story opens. She was kindly treated by her owners and her old mistress, who was very fond of her, taught her to sew and do housework and took such pains in teaching her that she became quite skilful in needlework and everything pertaining to housekeeping. Jane's lot was a pleasant one and until she reached the age of sixteen none of the evils of slavery shadowed her life. Then her old master died and she became the property of his son, who took possession of the premises and assumed the care of Jane's old mistress. This son was a wicked, thoughtless man and poor Jane was completely under his control. After living with him some time, she became the mother of a beautiful little girl, who was almost as white as her father, Jane's master.

Those who have seen quadroons and octoroons[32] will remember their peculiar style of beauty, the rich olive tint of the complexion, the large bright eyes, the perfect features and the long wavy black hair. A hundred romantic associations and mysterious fancies clustered around that class in the South, owned, as they often were, often by their own fathers and sold by them.

Jane was a house-servant and did not have to work under the lash or toil in the fields, as many slave-women were compelled to do, but she felt keenly the degradation of her position and longed to be free, that she might live a purer life. She had experienced a change of heart and become a Christian and this offended her master. He decided to sell her, when her little girl was about three years old. The old mistress was opposed to it, but her words had no effect; the master declared that he would sell Jane to the first trader that came along. Jane's mistress informed her of the fate in store for her and said that she longed to save her from it, but was powerless. Jane was greatly alarmed and in her distress went to tell her grief to an English family, who lived near by, kind-hearted people, who were opposed to slavery. They were much attached to Jenny, as they called her and felt great sympathy with her in her distress. The old gentleman went to see her master and tried to dissuade him from his purpose of selling Jane, but he could not be moved. Nothing was said about the child. The old gentleman told me afterward that he had no thought that the brute would sell his own child. Next day the old Englishman and his son-in-law concluded that by their united efforts they could raise a sum sufficient to purchase Jane, supposing that her master would sell her at a fair price. They went to him and offered him five hundred dollars for her, intending to secure her freedom and to allow her reasonable wages until she paid back the amount. But the master refused to take it. He said Jane was a handsome girl and would bring a high price down South; he would not take less than eight hundred dollars for her and thought perhaps he might get a thousand. This was more money than Jane's friends were able to give; they thought it was an unreasonable price and gave up the idea of buying her. A few days afterward the master sold Jane and her beautiful child to a Southern Negro-trader, receiving eleven hundred dollars for them both – nine hundred for the mother and two hundred for the child.

When Jane learned that she was sold, to be taken to the far South, her distress was indescribable. She and her little girl were to go together, but she knew not how soon they would be separated. She slipped into the house of her English friends, almost overwhelmed with grief and begged them to help her in some way, to save her from being sent away. They felt deeply for her distress, but what could they do? Jane was to have one day in which to wash and iron her clothes, then she must start away with her new master, the slave-trader.

The old Englishman concluded to go over to Cincinnati that day and see William Casey, a worthy coloured man of his acquaintance and counsel with him about Jane. Casey soon suggested a plan to get her over the river and put her on the Underground Railroad for Canada. The old man knew very little about the Underground Railroad, but he had full confidence in William Casey, knowing him to be a true and reliable man and agreed to carry out his suggestions if possible. Casey said he would get a skiff and go across the river in the early part of the night to a woodboat that lay at the bank in the lower part of Covington. The nights were then dark and he thought he could carry out his plan unmolested. The old Englishman was to apprise Jane of the plan and tell her to watch for an opportunity to slip out into a certain dark alley, where he would be in waiting. He would then conduct her to the woodboat where Casey agreed to be and she could be rowed across to the city under cover of darkness and secreted in some safe place.

Her English friend managed to communicate the plan to Jane and she watched diligently for an opportunity to escape, but she was kept busy, till late, washing and fixing her clothes preparatory to starting on her journey next day and her mistress or someone else stayed in the room to watch her.

Jane's heart throbbed with anxious excitement as the time drew near for the door to be closed and no opportunity offered for her to get away. She did not want to leave her little girl, but knew not how she could take her out of the house without exciting suspicion. She went into the yard several times in the evening and finally the child who had remained awake – something altogether unusual – followed her out. This was the very opportunity for which Jane had been watching and hoping and she did not let it pass. Taking her little daughter in her arms, she made her way into the back alley and walked rapidly toward the place where she was to meet her friend, the Englishman. The child, as if knowing that something was at stake, kept perfectly quiet.

Jane's friend was waiting at the rendezvous, though he had almost given her up and concluded that it was impossible for her to get away. Together they proceeded to the river, Jane trembling so much with excitement that she was obliged to give her child to her conductor to carry. Walking across to the wood-boat, the Englishman perceived a man waiting in a skiff and though it was too dark to distinguish faces, he felt

> ✛
> They were soon secreted in an upstairs room, where they remained in safety for several weeks
> ✛

confident that it was the faithful Casey and handed him the child. Then assisting Jane into the skiff, he bade her good-by, with a fervent 'God bless you!'

Casey brought the fugitives to our house, where they arrived about midnight. We knew nothing of the circumstances beforehand, but were accustomed to receive fugitives at all hours. They were soon secreted in an upstairs room, where they remained in safety for several weeks.

About a week after Jane's escape, the old Englishman, who had been afraid to make any inquiry before, came over to Cincinnati to learn what had become of her. He was not acquainted with the Underground Railroad and its workings and inquired of Casey whether its agents or managers were reliable persons. Casey told him there was a man in the city who could tell him all about it and also give him information regarding Jane. He then conducted him to our house, introduced him and told what his errand was.

I informed him that instead of the Underground Railroad being an institution organized for the purpose of making money, it was attended with great expense and explained the principles by which the managers were actuated and the motives which prompted us to spend our time and money in aiding the poor fugitives; which so affected the old man that he shed tears. Having answered his questions satisfactorily, I invited him to walk upstairs with me. I gave a light tap at Jane's door, which was locked and when it was opened, I introduced to Jane the friend and benefactor, to whom she owed her escape from slavery. Jane threw herself into the Englishman's arms and they both wept like children. Then he took up her lovely and interesting child and kissed it, after which he had a long conversation with her, giving her much good advice. When he bade her good-by and started away, he gave her five dollars.

Jane's master made great efforts to find her and the child and after a general and thorough search in the city, men were sent to the lake shore to watch at different points where fugitives were wont to take passage for Canada. He was heard to say that he intended to find her, if he had to put one foot in hell. When I heard of this expression I remarked that I feared he would get both feet there, but thought that he would not find Jane.

All this time she was safe and comfortable in her quarters at our house. She became much attached to 'Uncle Levy and Aunt Katy' as she called us and when the time came for her to leave she wept bitterly. She was put into the care of William Beard, that active agent for the Underground Railroad, who lived in Union County, Indiana and he took her to a coloured school in Randolph County, called the Union Literary Institute and there left her to attend school.

About this time, a young slave girl from the far South, who had made her way to the Mississippi River and there secreted herself on an up-river boat, by aid of a friend, arrived at Cincinnati and came to our house. After remaining here a short time, she was sent to the same school which Jane attended. They studied during the summer term and made fine progress, but in the autumn some of the coloured people of Cincinnati visited the school and I, fearing that the girls might be discovered – that the news of their whereabouts might reach their pursuers – went to the school and bade them prepare for travelling, explaining to them the exigencies of the occasion. They had become attached to the place and were reluctant to leave, but I told them that they would incur a great risk by remaining and they finally consented to go to Canada if I would accompany

> ✦
> She had married an industrious man of nearly her own colour and was comfortably situated and very happy
> ✦

them across the lake. I agreed to do so and we started together, but on the way I stopped at Oberlin, Ohio and had a meeting with the friends of fugitives there and as I could not well spare the time for the journey, a reliable and trustworthy gentleman offered to go in my stead. The girls being convinced that they could put entire confidence in this escort, excused me from the task and soon were on their way.

Some years afterwards I accompanied a party of fugitives to Amherstburg, Canada West, and there had the pleasure of dining with Jane in her own home. She had married an industrious man of nearly her own colour and was comfortably situated and very happy. If it had not been for the intervention of the friends of humanity she would doubtless have been toiling, broken-hearted, beneath the burning sun in Southern fields and of times fallen under the cruel sting of the lash instead of living in peace and happiness in her Northern home.

5

Dangerous Songs, Secret Messages

It was Year Zero for every person who was kidnapped and stolen from Africa.

Each man, woman and child left behind their name, family, home, language, culture, tradition and country.

Olaudah Equiano was born in 1745, an Ibo from the Eboe region of modern Nigeria. He was kidnapped and sold into slavery when he was ten years old. Years later, he wrote one of the most influential books on the slave trade, and recalled the voyage from Africa:

> I was soon put down under the docks, and there I received such a salutation in my nostrils as I had never experienced in my life: so that, with the loathsomeness of the stench, and crying together, I became so sick and low that I was not able to eat, nor had I the least desire to taste anything.
>
> I now wished for my last friend, death, to relieve me; but soon, to my grief, two of the white men offered me vegetables; and on my refusing to eat, one of them held me fast by the hand, and tied my feet, while the other flogged me severely.[33]

The journey from Africa to the Americas and the Caribbean could last anything from two to four months and Africans were treated brutally. Slaving ships were packed with between 250 and 600 Africans into the space between the cargo hold and the lower deck. The hold itself was tiny, and in many ships they were stacked like spoons, with no room to stand up, turn or move. The air in the hold was hot and stale and slaves had to lie in each other's urine, faeces and blood. In such cramped quarters, diseases spread quickly, with dysentery and small pox the main causes of death. Often, the living were chained to the dead, until the corpses were thrown overboard.

Anyone who survived the horrifying journey across the Atlantic was condemned to a lifetime of blood, sweat and tears. Africans were compelled to become a slave labour force for the European conquerors of the New World.

Slave-owners tried their best to destroy every trace of their slaves' culture. Families were split up, communicating instruments such as drums and horns were banned. Despite this, a sense of tradition, customs and languages lived on, particularly in their music.

> ✢
> Anyone who survived the horrifying journey across the Atlantic was condemned to a lifetime of blood, sweat and tears
> ✢

The slaves of Africa carried with them a rich culture that included, among other things, the tradition of singing. These people came from societies in which music was an important part of daily life. They were used to expressing ideas in songs and music-making was a natural part of their world.

Music carried many meanings. The rhythm gave the village folk who toiled in the field a driving movement and a sense of group dynamics. Songs helped the community pass on their history from one generation to another, celebrating anniversaries, achievements, epochs and special events; it conveyed emotions, similar to poetry and drama. Without a written language, the oral history tradition became an important instrument in African culture.

Plantation slaves, as we have seen, were divided into two groups: house servants and field slaves. It was the latter group that made up songs as they worked, picking cotton and working in the fields, laying railroad tracks, chopping wood or rowing. When the overseers allowed them, the field slaves would raise their voices and use clapped percussion as musical rhythms to make up work songs and field hollers as they timed their labour to the tempo of their singing.

Their songs reflected their experience of the toil and torment of slavery; picking cotton and working on the railroads became two important themes. Lawrence Levine remarked that the music went beyond expressing hope and despair and could be 'pervaded by a sense of change, transcendence, ultimate justice and personal worth.'

The slaves carried the songs and music of their respective homelands and found a temporary escape in music, expressing both hope and despair in their songs. Their music emphasized their love of God, a desire for freedom, total contempt for the institution of slavery and plans for secret meetings or escape.

As slaves accepted the Christian faith of their masters, the church became a regular part of their Sundays, their only day of rest and communal songs were popular, inspired by African musical traditions. The music was rhythmic, used hand-clapping, foot-stomping, dancing and shouting to accompany the harmonic singing, while the songs and lyrics were composed on the spot. The songs, characterized by traditional West African rhythmic and harmonic patterns, used a 'call and response' or leader-chorus model, in which a leader sang or chanted a few lines and the group repeated or suggested variations on the line in response. The leader spontaneously improvised text, timing and melody and the group responded with a short repetitive phrase. This style drew upon many of the practices fundamental to the African cultures the slaves had left behind, focusing on the importance of the spoken word, marking verbal improvisations and encouraging group participation.

The lyrics of slave songs expressed deep emotions about their plight. They were forbidden to sing about release and freedom but adapted the Old Testament story of Moses and the Israelites escape out of Egypt and this freedom protest became a recurring theme of many songs. They had hopes of being free and sang about such physical liberty in the context of a spiritual journey that took them towards freedom and these songs would create an inner freedom while the lyrics expressed their troubles, hopes and protests.

> ✦
> The lyrics of slave songs expressed deep emotions about their plight
> ✦

The soulful longing for their homeland was identified in this following lament:

> If me want for go in a Ebo
> Me can't go there!
> Since dem tief me from a Guinea
> Me can't go there!
> If me want for go in a Congo
> Me can't go there!
> Since dem tief me from my tatter
> Me can't go there!

If me want for go in a Baytown
Me can't go there!
Since massa go in a England
Me can't go there!

In *Captive Passage*, Linda Heywood commented, 'Even in the sad cadence of this song, defiance comes through. The creators of the song put the blame for their removal from their native communities squarely on the shoulders of the European slave traders and plantation owners, an interpretation that Creole folklore emphasized.'[34]

Slave-masters outlawed drums fearing that they were used to communicate to other captives; in reality, drummers could recreate the actual pitches of the words of Western African languages by striking different areas of the drum.

The drums of West African countries were the major instrument of the continent and the oldest original rhythmic instrument. Drums ranged in length from about twelve inches to as long as six or seven feet and in diameter from two or three inches to several feet. They were usually made from hollowed logs with animal skins tightened by pegs driven into the wood.

The slave musicians adapted English, Scottish and Irish folk tunes, sea shanties and hymns and these came to be called 'spiritual songs'. The term 'spiritual' was used for the first time when *Slave Songs of the United States* was published in 1867. It was the first ever such collection, with over one hundred sacred and secular slave songs including 'Roll Jordan Roll'; 'Michael Row the Boat Ashore'; 'Nobody Knows the Trouble I've Seen'; 'Come Go With Me'; 'Jacob's Ladder'; 'The Old Ship of Zion'; 'Run Nigger Run' and 'I Can't Stay Behind'.[35]

Many slave-owners encouraged their slaves to sing songs of faith. They reasoned that any slaves who turned

✦

Many slave-owners encouraged their slaves to sing songs of faith

✦

to religion were unlikely to be troublesome on earth. But their songs communicated messages understood only in their immediate circumstance, secrets hidden in everyday jargon, with codes that were intended to help the fugitive in their lonely journey into the unknown.

To the slave community, songs served another purpose. Because some unsuspecting slave-holders sanctioned group meetings for church-type services, Africans used songs to covertly discuss plans for escape and rebellion. Many of the songs carried hints, hidden messages, maps, double meanings and signals for slaves looking towards escape.

Frederick Douglass confirmed that he'd sung songs as a slave that used codes and secret message. He wrote:

> I thought I heard them say
> There were lions along the way
> I don't expect to stay
> Much longer here
> Run to Jesus – shun the danger
> I don't expect to stay
> Much longer here

> [This] was a favourite air and had a double meaning. In the lips of some, it meant the expectation of a speedy summons to the world of spirits; but in the lips of our company, it simply meant a speedy pilgrimage toward a free state and deliverance from all the evils and dangers of slavery.

'Steal Away' was a song of faith and fervour but also an invitation to the slaves to escape to freedom.

They sang of 'going home' or 'being bound for the land of Canaan' or 'crossing Jordan'. Anyone passing a group harmonizing might think they were singing about leaving their earthly home for a heavenly paradise. While this would have been an earnest desire, the song's hidden meaning was their hope of crossing the Ohio River and reaching the North where they would find freedom from slavery. The reference to 'Jordan' could be the Promised Land and 'paradise' but also Canada, where slavery was illegal. 'Canaan' sounded a lot like 'Canada'. 'Go Down Moses' might be a hint that Harriet Tubman was lurking in the shadows.

The very title of 'Wade in the Water' instructed runaways on how to avoid being tracked by bloodhounds. They should travel in the shallow waters of the river where the dogs wouldn't be able to pick up their scent:

> Wade in the water (children)
> Wade in the water
> Wade in the water
> God's gonna trouble the water
>
> If you don't believe I've been redeemed
> God's gonna trouble the water
> I want you to follow him on down to Jordan stream
> (I said) My God's gonna trouble the water
> You know chilly water is dark and cold
> (I know my) God's gonna trouble the water
> You know it chills my body but not my soul
> (I said my) God's gonna trouble the water
>
> (Come on let's) wade in the water
> Wade in the water (children)

Wade in the water
God's gonna trouble the water

Now if you should get there before I do
(I know) God's gonna trouble the water
Tell all my friends that I'm comin' too
(I know) God's gonna trouble the water
Sometimes I'm up Lord and sometimes I'm down
(You know my) God's gonna trouble the water
Sometimes I'm level to the ground
God's gonna trouble the water
(I know) God's gonna trouble the water

Wade in the water (children)
Wade out in the water (children)
God's gonna trouble the water

The spiritual, 'Swing Low, Sweet Chariot' used the call and response idea with people/fugitives waiting for help. 'I looked over Jordan and what did I see/coming for to carry me home/a band of angels coming after me.' The way home was by riding a 'chariot' or a 'train'.

'Swing Low, Sweet Chariot' was associated with Harriet Tubman, who apparently sang the song as she lay dying, with her family gathered at her bedside.

+

'Follow the Drinking Gourd' was the most famous secret song with the words referring to an escape route

+

The words of 'The Gospel Train' declared 'She is coming . . . Get on board . . . there's room for many more.' This is a clear call to leave by riding a train which stops at stations.

'Follow the Drinking Gourd' was the most famous secret song with the words referring to an escape route. The coded lyrics contained elements of a map that directed people to significant points along the escape route. The song carried detailed instructions and ended with advice that they must cross over to the North side of the big Ohio River where someone would ensure their passage to a safe house, the first step of their journey to freedom in Canada. The title itself was a veiled reference to the Big Dipper which pointed to the North Star and freedom:

When the sun goes back
and the first quail calls
Follow the drinking gourd
The old man is a-waitin' for
to carry you to freedom
Follow the drinking gourd

Chorus
Follow the drinking gourd,
follow the drinking gourd
For the old man is a-waitin'
to carry you to freedom
Follow the drinking gourd

The river bed makes a mighty fine road,
Dead trees to show you the way
And it's left foot, peg foot, travelling on
Follow the drinking gourd

The river ends between two hills
Follow the drinking gourd
There's another river on the other side
Follow the drinking gourd

I thought I heard the angels say
Follow the drinking gourd
The stars in the heavens
gonna show you the way
Follow the drinking gourd

+

The exact original meaning of the codes in these songs have probably been lost to history

+

The song's first commercially released recording was by the Weavers in 1951 and Lee Hays told Pete Seeger, both members of the popular folk group, that he first heard it in 1916–1920. It was used by the Civil Rights movement and has been recorded almost two hundred times.

While the exact original meaning of the codes in these songs have probably been lost to history, it's not hard to imagine how such music was used at the time.

Kim and Reggie Harris have kept the tradition alive through their CDs and performances and have offered these comments on particular songs:

Let us break bread together on our knees: A coded call for a secret meeting or gathering in the morning (at or before sunrise) to discuss issues of concern, plans of escape or for a time of prayer.

No more auction block for me: Desperate to escape the whip, the degradation of the slave auction, family separation and inhuman conditions, this song most often would be sung under one's breath, out of earshot of master or overseer, as a statement of purpose or defiance.

Go down Moses: Slaves understood the message of the Bible story of Moses leading his people to freedom in a way that slave-owners often overlooked. In a marvellous example of coded language, they could sing about this story right in front of the master. The name Moses might refer to the biblical character or to a 'conductor' (Harriet Tubman). Pharaoh (the slave-holder) would not expect Israel (the slaves) to make an attempt to leave Egypt (bondage) for the Promised Land (freedom).

Runaway Slaves in Canada

When Josiah Henson decided to escape from his slave-owner, he set his sights on one place only: Canada.

On his master's plantation in Maryland, Frederick Douglass joined other slaves in singing about the joys of Canaan and heaven, but he wrote later that Canada was always on his mind.

Canada was the intended destination of every runaway slave. But how would they be welcomed after they crossed the border?

The French had brought the first slaves to Canada around 1608 but the first recorded slave purchase in the country was a young boy from Madagascar, who had been taken to Quebec by British Commander David Kirke in 1628. The boy was sold to the head clerk of the French colony and was baptized in 1633 as Olivier Le Jeune, taking the name of the French clerk and the surname of the French priest, who established the school where he was taught. By the time of his death in 1654, Olivier Le Jeune's official status had changed from that of domestic servant to freeman.

In the eighteenth century, immigrants from Britain could apply for a portion of land to farm and labourers were imported as slaves. At the time, Canada was made up of six separate British colonies with a population of less than three million people.

While the French preferred to use 'panis' who were Native Americans of Pawnee descent, the English settlers brought in African slaves. Governor Denonville had sought royal permission to import slaves directly from Africa but this request was denied in 1688 and a direct slave trade from Africa to Canada was never established. By 1759, there were about 3,604 recorded slaves, of whom 1,132 were Africans. Of the total brought to Canada, about 40 per cent were female and 60 per cent male. Most of the slaves in Canada were servants acquired by wealthy families and usually served the same master during their lifetime.

The first shots of the American War of Independence were fired on 19 April 1775 in Massachusetts, the most rebellious of the thirteen British colonies. This relatively minor skirmish quickly escalated as news of the revolt spread and, the following year, the Declaration of Independence was signed. The British were determined to do everything to upset the rebels and promised freedom to any American slave who abandoned their owners and joined the British forces. In *Bury the Chains*, Adam Hochschild reported that the first three hundred Africans were enlisted as the Royal Ethiopian Regiment and handed uniforms which carried the words 'Liberty to Slaves'. Hochschild wrote, 'This promise by the British did not come from wanting to end slavery, of course; it was merely a strategic manoeuvre to deprive the enemy of property.'[36]

When the Declaration of Independence was signed in 1776, slavery was legal in all thirteen colonies. The slogan 'All men are created equal' proved paradoxical when the champions of liberty were themselves slave-owners, including George Washington, Thomas Jefferson and Benjamin Franklin. It was a tragic contradiction at the very heart of the American Revolution. Clearly, some citizens were more equal than others.

Franklin owned slaves for thirty years and sold them at his general store. Later his ideas changed: he started the first African school and he argued for their freedom.

The British tactics worked and slaves fled their masters' plantations to cross into British lines; even George Washington's slaves ran away to join the British.

The War of Independence began as a civil war but turned into an international conflict when France, Spain and the Netherlands joined the rebels in the colonies in their fight for freedom from Britain. The French support proved decisive to the subsequent American victory, eight and a half years later, in 1783.

✦

When the Declaration of Independence was signed in 1776, slavery was legal in all thirteen colonies

✦

About 3,500 slaves who'd been promised freedom were taken to Canada by the British in 1783. They were settled in segregated communities in Nova Scotia and New Brunswick but the land and terrain proved unsuitable and the initiative broke down.

Thomas Peters emerged as a leader in the African community, an unsung hero, curiously hidden from history, yet named by Simon Schama as the first identifiable African-American political leader. In *Rough Crossings*, Schama noted that Peters was enslaved by the French, then taken to Louisiana, where he was flogged and branded for repeated attempts at escaping. When the British flare went up for slaves to join their forces, he fled his owner's flour mill in North Carolina and joined the Black Pioneers, another regiment set up by the British.[37]

Peters was determined to fight for their rights and he was disturbed that little progress had been made in Canada. After seven years, the former slaves were still living in the hard terrain of Nova Scotia on meagre government rations, battling a bitterly cold environment and prejudice, with the promise of land by the British unequally dispersed and still largely unfulfilled. Somehow he found the courage to take up the challenge.

He set sail for England to seek help for his people with the knowledge that he was putting himself in extreme danger. Peters was still a slave in America and if he was betrayed by anyone on his journey and forcibly returned to the United States, he would be immediately sold into slavery.

But his mission to London in 1791 proved successful, gaining the support of the black community, then the abolitionists and finally the government. It was through Peters that Granville Sharpe got involved. Thomas Clarkson's brother, John, took an active part, with Peters in getting over eleven hundred former slaves to join him and leave Nova Scotia for Sierra Leone and, in 1792, they founded Freetown. In *Rough Crossings*, Schama concluded, 'The story in the end turned to one of tragedy, where the idea of a free black country became subsumed by the British promises that were eventually hedged and qualified. In 1808, Sierra Leone became just another imperial colony.'

Meanwhile, in Canada, slaves continued to be bought and sold until a determined abolitionist, John Graves Simcoe, a former owner of Hemyock Castle in Devon, was appointed governor of Upper Canada (modern Ontario). He successfully introduced a bill in 1793 that proposed gradual emancipation and this became the only British colony to legislate for the abolition of slavery. It stopped slaves being imported, though all living slaves would remain with their masters. Any children born of slaves would become free when they turned twenty-five and their children would be 'born free'.

✦

It stopped slaves being imported, though all living slaves would remain with their masters

✦

This pioneering legislation didn't free any slaves as it proposed gradual abolition but it did save thousands of lives and ironically had its greatest impact south of the border, in the United States, as it sent a clear signal to slaves that they could win their freedom if they could cross the border and reach Canada.

That same year (1793), the US Congress passed a new law, the first Fugitive Slave Act, making it a criminal offence for anyone to help a runaway slave or to prevent their arrest.

Canada was attacked in 1812, when the United States declared war on Britain and again the British offered land and freedom to American blacks who would join the English side, just as they had done during the American Revolution. This time, the US lost but, once again, the land that the British allocated to the slaves proved unworkable.

In *North Star to Freedom*, Gena Gorrell reported that in 1819, the American government asked Canada to return runaway slaves and for permission to hunt down escaped fugitive slaves on Canadian soil.[38] The request was denied.

At the time, many campaigners and politicians such as Abraham Lincoln and William Wilberforce supported 'gradual abolition' as the accepted route for slavery to be demolished. In *Jubilee*, Howard Dodson observed, 'During the colonial period, only the enslaved Africans consistently called for the abolition of slavery through word and deed. The first and most consistent abolitionists were those enslaved Africans who said slavery was wrong.'[39]

Simon Schama, in *Rough Crossings*, spotlighted the black tailor, David Walker, in Boston, who published his *Appeal to the Coloured Citizens of the World* in 1829.[40] Schama said it was 'an incendiary attack on the hypocrisy of the United States for purporting to establish itself on the principles of liberty and equality while continuing to deny them to three million slaves.' According to Jessica McElrath, author of an online African-American History Guide, Walker attacked Thomas Jefferson's arguments that blacks were inferior to whites and used Christian terminology and theology to assert that slavery was a sin. Walker was one of the first activists to call for the total abolition of slavery worldwide. At the time, the abolitionists favoured gradual abolition or colonization. He also urged slaves to use violence if necessary to win their freedom.

The British Parliament abolished slavery in the British Empire in 1833, including the Canadian colonies, and Emancipation Day was celebrated every year with parades, church services, banquets, speeches and football games to mark the historic event. In fact, the Act took effect from 1 August 1834 and awarded compensation of £20 million paid not to slaves but to slave-owners for the loss of their property. Parliament also decided that all enslaved Africans would have to work for their owners

✦

The British Parliament abolished slavery in the British Empire in 1833

✦

as 'apprentices' for twelve years before they could be freed. After pressure, this period was eventually reduced to four years. The true end of slavery came five years later on 1 August 1838, when nearly one million African men, women and children throughout the British Empire were no longer enslaved and became officially free.

After 'emancipation' in 1833, there was only one recorded incident in Canadian history when the law failed to protect a black refugee. In 1856, two Canadian magistrates conspired with US officials in the secret capture of Archy Lanton and his transportation back to his owner in the American South. Both magistrates were immediately fired from their posts.

Sixteen years after slavery was abolished in Canada, the United States passed the second Fugitive Slave Act in 1850 and this gave slave-owners, slave-catchers and bounty-hunters the right to track down and capture fugitives anywhere in America. Canada became the land of dreams for every slave in the country. It also led directly to a time of intense activity for the conductors and members of the Underground Railroad.

Runaway slaves like Josiah Henson who eventually reached the safety of Canada's borders were met with a mixed reception. Some were denied permission to buy land while others were forced to leave land that they had already worked on. Significantly, they were equal in the eyes of the law and could challenge discrimination and prejudice in court. Over time, they proved diligent workers and established productive and successful communities.

The first large group of runaway slaves arrived in Canada between 1817 and 1820 and settled in Essex County, chosen because it was the easiest place to reach from the American border. Underground Railroad supporters in Ontario were active on Lake Erie and the

Niagara River, as well as Amhertsburg, Sandwich, Windsor, Owen Sound, Hamilton, St Catharines, Toronto, Kingston, Brantford, Collingwood and Prescott, and settlements were found near the cities of Chatham, Hamilton, Windsor, London, Toronto and St. Catharine's. Smaller settlements were located near Barrie, Guelph and Owen Sound. Ships such as *Bay City, United States, Arrow, Mayflower, Forest Queen, May Queen, Morning Star* and *Phoebus* would let fugitives on board and drop them without charge on Canadian soil.

An 1850 Sandwich newspaper article stated that there were 24,000–30,000 Africans living in Canada. The African journalist Mary Ann Shadd put the figure at 35,000 after the passing of the Slave Fugitive Act five years later, though the author of *Bound for Canaan* quoted a modern source who studied the census records of the period and concluded that in 1861 there were probably about 23,000 blacks in all of Canada West.

The African slaves drifted towards communities where black families had settled to avoid discrimination and to gain protection from American bounty-hunters. By the 1850s, there were six established settlements in Ontario including one called Dawn led by Josiah Henson near Dresden. This group had a school and a commercial sawmill, where immigrants were given some training and an education.

✦

Larwill accused blacks of being inferior and warned home owners that property values would fall if they settled in the community

In 1849, an Irish Christian minister called William King persuaded the Presbyterian Church to assist a slave community in Chatham, Ontario, but the project had fierce opposition from Edwin Larwill, an important local merchant and editor of the *Chatham Journal*. Larwill accused blacks of being inferior and warned home owners that property values would fall if they settled in the community. Larwill threatened that allowing runaway slaves to settle in Canada could provoke a war with America and demanded that all Africans should be forced to pay a poll tax, barred from voting and eventually forced to return to the United States.

Reverend King was warned that his life was in danger from Larwill and his vigilante committee and their supporters. But King wouldn't back down.

At one public meeting held at the Royal Exchange Hotel in Chatham, King faced a hostile crowd who booed his plans for the African community and school for the children of runaway slaves. King needed an armed guard of a dozen black men and had only one other white man, Archibald McKellar, by his side.

Local churches provided money while the new African settlers did all the work and eventually the Elgin settlement emerged. Under King's guidance, the school was a resounding success with white children competing for places. It proved to be the best school in the region.

The settlement prospered as Elgin's farmers profited from rich harvests and this enabled settlers to pay off their mortgages in record time.

Finally, in 1857, voters evicted the racist Larwill from Parliament and instead voted in Archibald McKellar as the new Member of Parliament, the man who had stood shoulder to shoulder with Reverend King when the new settlement was planned. Larwill had been defeated by almost eight hundred votes, the biggest margin ever recorded in the district.

Graduates from Reverend King's school in Elgin went on to make their mark: Jerome Riley became a medical doctor and established the first Freedmen's hospital in

Washington DC, during the Civil War. William Rapier made it to Congress, while other graduates became teachers in local schools.

Not all slave communities achieved such results as some former slaves struggled to evade prejudice and pressures – but there were many other notable successes:

> **Delos Rogest Davis** was born in the slave state of Maryland but arrived in Canada at the age of four. He worked his way up and studied law and in 1884 a special Act was passed to enable him to become Canada's first black lawyer. In 1910, Davis was named 'King's Counsel', the first African to be given this honour in the British Empire.

> **Mary Ann Shadd** started teaching at Quaker-run schools in the United States when she was just sixteen and moved to Canada in 1850 when the second Slave Fugitive Act was passed. She published a booklet explaining the benefits of Canada's opportunities and urged American blacks to move North. In 1853, she became editor and business manager of a newspaper, the *Provincial Freeman*, probably the first woman in Canada to hold such a position. She graduated as a lawyer in 1883, becoming only the second black woman in the United States to earn a law degree at the time.

> **William Hall** was born in Nova Scotia in 1828 and went to sea at the age of twelve. He served in the Crimean War and sailed with the Royal Navy. In 1857, he helped a British garrison under siege in Lucknow, India and was awarded the Victoria Cross for his courage and bravery.

> **Elijah McCoy's** parents escaped from Kentucky with help from the Underground Railroad and he was born in

Canada. McCoy eventually returned to the United States and served as a railroad mechanical engineer. One of his inventions was an automatic lubricator for oiling the steam engines of locomotives, factory engines and transatlantic steamers. It was so superior that it became known as 'the real McCoy', and entered the global vocabulary as a popular catchphrase.

The War that Ended Slavery

Abraham Lincoln's election as President of the United States on 6 November 1860 enraged the South. The Republican Party had made anti-slavery its central platform and many Southerners felt that they didn't belong in the Union. By February the following year, seven Southern states had split and created the Confederate States of America.

The economy of the Southern states was based on crops like cotton, coffee, sugar, rice and tobacco and depended on a labour force to operate the plantations where the produce was grown. The Northern states had become industrialized and didn't need slaves for their economy. Demand for cotton both in America and overseas had increased and plantation owners relied on its slave force for success. The North wanted to abolish slavery but argued over equality for freed slaves and whether or not they should be equal to white people.

The US Census of 1860 revealed that 448,070 of the

> ✦
> Demand for cotton both in America and overseas had increased and plantation owners relied on its slave force for success
> ✦

4.4 million people of African descent in the US were free. Over 3.9 million were enslaved.

In Lincoln's inaugural address, on 4 March 1861, he declared that his duty was to preserve the Union. His political views were clear; he had no intention of ending slavery where it existed, or of repealing the Fugitive Slave Law. Lincoln favoured an amendment to the Constitution that guaranteed that slavery could never be abolished by future Congresses. He was a member of the American Colonization Society, with an objective to return all slaves to Africa, a popular opinion in the North.

Slavery was a troubling dilemma for Lincoln. He detested the idea that one person could have ownership of another, but the Southern states had been guaranteed the right to be slave holders and he didn't want to break that promise. He thought that freedom should come gradually, though he realized that the ideas of slavery and freedom were doomed to clash. He wrote, 'They are like two wild beasts in sight of each other, but chained and apart.'

On 12 April 1861, one month after Lincoln's inaugural address, Confederate troops opened fire on Fort Sumter, a military outpost off the coast of Charleston, South Carolina. These were the gun shots that signalled that the Civil War had officially begun.

Lincoln maintained that he was fighting the Civil War to preserve the Union but leaders such as Frederick Douglass insisted that the war couldn't be secured without abolishing slavery. He wrote, 'The war now being waged in this land is a war for and against slavery and it can never effectively be put down till one or the other of these vital forces is completely destroyed.'

The abolitionists wanted Lincoln to declare an end to slavery throughout the states but the President refused as he believed freedom should be ushered in gradually.

His political strategy was to seek to hold onto the four slave-holding states that were in the Union. In *North Star to Freedom*, Gena Gorrell explained, 'In 1862, he chose a compromise: he declared that slaves in the rebel Southern states were free, but he did nothing for the slaves in the loyal border states.'[41]

In September 1862, one year after the war had started, Lincoln issued a Preliminary Emancipation Proclamation that declared that all slaves would be freed. It also signalled that slavery was an important factor in the war. Lincoln's Proclamation, scholar Howard Dodson noted, 'marked the first time in American history that the US government had gone on record in favour of abolishing slavery anywhere.'

The Civil War was punishing and on 9 April 1865, the Confederate army surrendered.

Three million people had taken up weapons and six hundred thousand had died in the conflict that lasted four years. It was the greatest war in American history and was the only war fought on American soil by Americans.

✦
Three million people had taken up weapons and six hundred thousand had died in the conflict that lasted four years
✦

The Civil War put an end to slavery in America and nearly four million slaves were freed, over 12 per cent of the total population of the United States, according to the Census of 1860. About half a million slaves imported over the centuries had grown to a population of nearly four million. New laws were introduced to dismantle the institution of slavery, though in practice, Africans found that America wasn't that swift or willing to award them civil rights.

There were other disappointments.

When the Civil War started, Africans weren't allowed to enlist into either the Union or Confederate Army, but after Lincoln's Emancipation Proclamation in 1862, they were free to enlist on the Union side. They proved loyal and capable soldiers, after the first black regiment, the Fifty-fourth Massachusetts Volunteers attacked Fort Wagner, South Carolina, in July 1863.

About two hundred thousand black soldiers served in the Union Army and Navy, but they were forbidden to march in the official Grand Review in Washington, DC, parade and in places such as Philadelphia, they were denied the opportunity to march in the city's welcome home parade.

Harriet Tubman served the war effort as scout, spy and nurse. She was denied a pension.

Runaways and Songs of Slavery

The transatlantic slave trade was the largest international business of its time and the slaves of Africa provided the labour force that drove the new global financial systems which had evolved as a result.

Over four centuries of the slave trade, between nine and fifteen million slaves were sold and shipped as slaves in 54,000 slave voyages to service the international global trade that prospered the economies of all slave-trading nations.

Transatlantic slavery transformed the world beyond anything anyone could comprehend. After this, no one was untouched by the institution of slavery and it is central to our understanding of how our modern world developed.

Essentially, the slaves of Africa developed all slaving nations and contributed to their wealth and success.

In England, the profits from slavery flowed through most levels of society and establishments: the Bank of England, Lloyds of London, the British Museum, the National Gallery and the Anglican Church, among others. Slavery became the focal point of Britain's political economy and was accepted both socially and culturally, with the endorsement of the church. The investors in the slave trade included royalty, politicians, church leaders, and prominent figures of the day. Anyone who had a buck. Anyone who wanted to make a buck.

> ✦
> Slavery became the focal point of Britain's political economy and was accepted both socially and culturally
> ✦

For the slaves, it was devastating. They would never return home or see their families again. Their daily experience became an endless drudge of brutal service; it was the only life they knew.

While dynasties were forged in Europe and the Americas, families were destroyed in Africa. The human cost was unimaginable.

Yet the spirit of many African slaves would not be broken, no matter what torment or humiliation was inflicted on them. That spirit of resistance was evident through these extraordinary and compelling stories of escape, full of creativity, courage and inventiveness. These epic stories, virtually a hidden history, kept that spirit alive in their hearts and in the hearts of all those left behind on those plantations and fields and houses and shacks in America's southern states.

It was also preserved in their songs and music.

The slaves kept the idea of freedom alive in their hearts. They sang about physical freedom in the context of their faith. They accepted the Christian faith on their own terms, developing their own style of worship and church services. They believed that God had granted them spiritual freedom and would someday release their chains of slavery.

Such early songs of freedom that became the blues and spirituals that we sing and play today, were born of the deepest pain, cruelty and anguish, while the cries of the oppressed offered profound expressions of simple faith. Sometimes it was just a line repeated over and over, just a wordless lament, a moan, never better expressed than the ethereal elegy of Blind Willie Johnson's 'Dark was the Night, Cold was the Ground'.

This music reaches out to us from the past. It is compelling and haunting and moves us beyond anything we can comprehend; it stirs and connects us to each other and to God in a way that only such genuine expressions can ever do.

The music was both empowering and illuminating to those who created it, and retains the same qualities and power for those who discover it decades later. Over time, it would change the musical landscape of all popular modern music. It is simply an extraordinary legacy.

PART TWO

LEGACY

6

The Musical Heritage of Slave Songs

The Civil War brought an end to the institution of slavery in the American South. It did not deliver justice and equality to its former slaves.

On 16 January 1865, Major General William Sherman issued Special Field Order No. 15 awarding compensation of forty acres and a mule to former slaves and, by June, about ten thousand slaves had settled in Georgia and South Carolina. After Lincoln's assassination, his successor, Andrew Johnson, revoked the order. The slaves were ejected and the land returned to its former owners.

The Oscar-winning classic *Gone with the Wind* carried a brief scene that showed freed slaves getting the news. Jessy Dixon's new song '40 Acres and a Mule' echoes references about this broken promise from Public Enemy, George Clinton, Gil Scott-Heron, Nas, Kanye West and the late Tupac Shakur. Film-maker Spike Lee named his production company '40 Acres and a Mule Filmworks' to serve as a reminder of America's unpaid debt to its slave ancestors.

After the Civil War, the Jim Crow laws, which implemented strict, legalized segregation of the races, branded the future: 'Separate but Equal'. Treated as second-class citizens, blacks were separated from whites by law and by private action in transportation, public accommodations, recreational facilities, prisons, the armed forces and schools in both Northern and Southern states.

When Africans were given the vote in 1870, some states insisted that this should be limited to those who could read; ridiculous literacy tests were introduced at a time when 97 per cent of Africans were illiterate. Southern states added a 'Grandfather Clause' restricting rights to those with freed grandparents. The clause was established in 1895 and seven states clung to this law until the Supreme Court declared it unconstitutional, both in 1915 and again in 1939.

Beyond the law, however, there was always the threat of violence against blacks in the South who attempted to challenge or even question the established order. The Ku Klux Klan, the Knights of the White Camellia and other similar organizations murdered thousands of blacks (and some whites) in order to prevent blacks from voting or participating in public life.

Between 1884 and 1900 white mobs lynched more than two thousand blacks in the South. During World War I (1914–1918), lynching decreased slightly, but between 1900 and 1920 Southern whites lynched more than one thousand blacks. Many were alleged criminals, but blacks were also lynched for any violation of the code of Southern race relations such as talking to a white woman, attempting to vote or seeming to make trouble. Lynch mobs not only hanged blacks but also burned them alive, shot them, or just beat them to death.

+

Between 1884 and 1900 white mobs lynched more than two thousand blacks in the South

+

America's last mass lynching occurred on 25 July 1946 when a mob shot two black couples in Walton County, Georgia. The story became national news but no one was ever charged with the murders.

Spirituals Create a Sensation

Fisk University opened in Nashville, Tennessee in 1866 as the first American university to accept freed slaves. It hit a financial crisis five years later and a nine-member musical group called the Fisk Jubilee Singers organized a fund-raising tour in 1871 for their institution. This was the first time that most people beyond their own community had heard plantation songs or spirituals by African singers and they were a smash hit, first in America and later in Europe. After a successful tour in the United Kingdom in 1891, a member of the troupe settled in Yorkshire for the remaining twenty-four years of his life.

Spirituals developed into a sophisticated art form and became an international musical phenomenon, heard in the White House, the world's best concert halls and, later, Hollywood movies. Even Queen Victoria declared herself a fan. She wrote in her journal, 'They are real Negroes. They come from America and have been slaves. They sing extremely well together.'

First Black Classical Composer

One of the musical arrangers behind the 'spirituals sensation' that was taking the world by storm was Harry Burleigh. His slave grandfather, Hamilton Waters, had been blinded after a savage beating but had passed on his songs and love of music to his grandchild, who became a protégé of the noted classical composer, Antonín Dvořák. The Czech musician had agreed to head a prestigious musical academy in New York City and was fascinated by America and captivated by the music and culture of African-Americans and Native Americans. In 'Music in America', he wrote, 'I am convinced that the future music of this country must be founded on what are called Negro melodies. These can be the foundation of a serious and original school of composition, to be developed in the United States. These beautiful and varied themes are the product of the soil. They are the folk songs of America and your composers must turn to them.'[42]

Burleigh's talent was recognized and quickly came to Dvořák's attention. His son, Harry Burleigh II, noted that his father 'played and sang the old melodies for Dvořák such as "Swing Low, Sweet Chariot" which is mirrored in the second theme of the first movement of Dvořák's New World Symphony.'

Burleigh became a linguist, singing in Hebrew, Latin, Italian, French and German, and wrote and arranged a wide range of songs including 'Deep River' and 'Little Mother of Mine', sung throughout the world by John McCormack. He was a vocal coach for Caruso and the musical arranger for performers such as Paul Robeson and Marian Anderson, who created a worldwide demand for the songs that had their roots in slavery.

The Voice that Challenged America

Marian Anderson was born with the gift of music and the curse of racism. At twenty-one, she was refused entry to an all-white music school because of her colour. The woman at the admissions counter said bluntly, 'We don't take coloureds.' But her extraordinary musical talent eventually triumphed and she achieved worldwide recognition. She became so popular, that sometimes she would perform at three different places in a single night.

In 1939 when her manager, Sol Hurok, tried to book Washington's Constitutional Hall for a concert, the director slammed the phone down with the words, 'No Negro will ever appear in this hall while I am manager.'

The ban sparked a furore and eventually, Mrs Eleanor Roosevelt sponsored a free open-air concert at the Lincoln Memorial before around seventy-five thousand people and millions of radio listeners. In her autobiography, *My Lord, What a Morning*, Anderson wrote about the event: 'I said yes, but the yes did not come easily or quickly. I don't like a lot of show, and one could not tell in advance what direction the affair would take. I studied my conscience . . . As I thought further, I could see that my significance as an individual was small in this affair. I had become, whether I like it or not, a symbol, representing my people.'[43]

✦
At twenty-one, she was refused entry to an all-white music school because of her colour
✦

Several weeks later, President and Mrs. Roosevelt invited Anderson to sing for their guests, King George VI and Queen Elizabeth of Britain, at the White House, making her the first African-American to entertain there. In 1961, Anderson returned to Washington to sing the national anthem at President John F. Kennedy's inauguration.

African Worship

In 1890, the Church of God in Christ, the most popular black church opened in Mississippi and similar churches were to have a huge influence across the musical landscape. These churches continued African traditions from plantation services with hand clapping and 'call and response' styles of worship. With the end of World War II and with greater affluence, the market for Gospel 'race records' increased; groups and quartets were popular with a focus on the lead singer and the role of the soloist evolved. In the 1950s, the bass guitar took the role of a bass singer, and the role of choirs increased while composers arranged spirituals in a new way.

> ✦
> These churches continued African traditions from plantation services with hand clapping and 'call and response' styles of worship
> ✦

Musical Pioneer

One of the most influential musicians to break new ground was Charles Tindley, the son of a slave, in Maryland. He moved to Philadelphia where he undertook menial jobs while teaching himself to read and write. He completed his education and became a Methodist minister of the church he had once served as a janitor. A man of great faith, he once told his wife to set their dinner table even though there was no food or money in the house. Shortly afterwards, there was a knock on the door. A friend explained that they had cooked too much food and had brought some of it to share with the couple.

Tindley composed both words and music and was one of the first to publish and copyright his songs. His gospel hymn 'I'll Overcome Someday' merged with the spiritual 'I'll Be All Right' and the synthesis produced the anthem of the Civil Rights movement 'We Shall Overcome'. He wrote nearly fifty songs, including 'We'll Understand it Better By and By', 'Leave it There', 'The Storm is Passing Over', 'I Know the Lord Will Make a Way', 'What Are They Doing in Heaven', 'Without Him' (recorded by Elvis Presley) and 'Stand By Me' taken into the charts by Ben E. King and the Drifters.

Although Tindley composed most of his songs between 1901–1906, his music only became popular decades later. In 1921, one of his songs, 'I Do, Don't You', electrified the National Baptist Convention held at the Pilgrim Baptist Church in Chicago. Sitting in the congregation at the time was Thomas Dorsey, who said he had never been so moved in his life.

Gospel Music Legend

Thomas Dorsey was a Blues pianist known as 'Georgia Tom' who played barrel-house piano in a speak easy controlled by Al Capone in Chicago. He also played in Ma Rainey's Wild Cats Jazz Band, accompanied Bessie Smith and recorded a best-selling hit 'Tight Like That', with Tampa Red in 1928. After his wife and childhood sweetheart died in childbirth, Dorsey turned to the piano for solace and wrote 'Precious Lord, Take My Hand' in 1932 and, later, he composed 'Peace in the Valley' for Mahalia Jackson.

Spirituals and the Blues charted parallel lines in popular and sacred music. Thomas Dorsey played both sides of the street. He had enjoyed commercial success but then followed his father, a Baptist preacher, into the church and his musical instincts found creative expression in an emerging new form of music. It is thought that Ira Sankey coined the term 'Gospel Music' in 1875 but its popularity in the 1930s was due to the dynamism of Thomas Dorsey's Gospel songs. Gospel reflected the concerns of urban life and was the creative musical juggernaut

✦

Spirituals and the Blues charted parallel lines in popular and sacred music

✦

that moved the rural traditions of folk spirituals into modern times. Dorsey set up the first publishing firm to promote Black Gospel performers and became the first independent publisher of this new form. His background in the Blues influenced his writing of Gospel songs and he was at the forefront of the movement that linked Gospel with Blues.

From the Church to the Charts

Mixing the sacred and secular created immediate tensions but by the end of the 1930s, Gospel music renewed African-Americans' commitment to the Church and provided a platform for brilliant young musicians, many of whom later pursued successful careers in the music business. Popular music reaped the benefit.

Sister Rosetta Tharpe took the Gospel beat out of the church halls when she played with Cab Calloway at the Cotton Club in Harlem in the early 1930s. In 1938, Tharpe became the first Gospel singer to record for a secular label, Decca, and the following year hit the pop charts with 'This Train'.

In 1952, Clyde McPhatter and the Dominoes replaced 'Lord' with 'baby' on 'Have Mercy, Baby', and this concept was repeated on several hit records. 'This Little Light of Mine' became 'This Little Girl of Mine'. 'Stand by Me', 'Save the Last Dance for Me' and 'Under the Boardwalk' used the same bass line and harmonies as 'God is Standing By' by the Soul Stirrers, while the lead singer of the group, Sam Cooke, went on to huge commercial success.

7

The Birth of the Blues

In 1903, W.C. Handy, a local band-leader, was waiting for a train in Tutwiler, Mississippi, when he was startled by another black man singing.[44]

The man was in rags, his feet peeped out of his shoes and his face was etched with the sadness of the ages. He played a beat-up guitar and used a knife to slide up and down the neck of the instrument. He repeated one line three times:

> Going where the Southern crosses the Dog
> Going where the Southern crosses the Dog
> Going where the Southern crosses the Dog

It was a reference to a nearby intersection of two railways, the Southern Railroad and the Yazoo Delta Railroad (nicknamed the Yellow Dog), suggesting that he had made up the song himself. The troubadour had no explanation for what he was playing; Handy described it as 'the weirdest music I had ever

✦
'Each one of my Blues is based on some old Negro song of the South'
✦

heard'. Later, Handy named the music and promoted the style. He called it 'the Blues'.

Handy based his band at Pee Wee's Saloon on Memphis's notorious Beale Street. He wrote a commercial for the city mayor's successful campaign and in 1912 turned the jingle into 'Memphis Blues', the first song to include 'Blues' in its title. By 1917, Handy had moved to New York and three of his most famous songs had been published as sheet music: 'Memphis Blues', 'St Louis Blues' and 'Beale Street Blues'.

The music created a sensation. 'Memphis Blues' had a dance, the fox trot, named after it. 'St Louis Blues' was turned into a Hollywood film; England's King Edward VIII once asked Scottish bagpipers to play it for him; in the 1930s, when Italy invaded Ethiopia, it became the Ethiopian battle hymn.

Handy was an entertainer and was clear about the origins of his songs. 'Each one of my Blues is based on some old Negro song of the South . . . Something that sticks in my mind, that I hum to myself when I'm not thinking about it. Some old song that is a part of the memories of my childhood and of my race. I can tell you the exact song I used as a basis for any one of my Blues.'

In *Father of the Blues*, Handy wrote, 'My parents were among the four million slaves who had been freed and left to shift for themselves. I was born in a log cabin which my grandfather had built.'[45]

In slavery days, Handy's grandfather and his two brothers escaped using the Underground Railroad; one brother reached Canada, the other made it to the east 'but my grandfather was overtaken and sold into slavery in Alabama where, still urged by the desire for freedom, he started an insurrection for escape and was shot but not killed.'

After gaining his freedom, Handy's grandfather became a Methodist minister and built the first 'coloured' church in his hometown of Florence, Alabama, the town where William Christopher was born in 1873.

Handy's father's brother, Hanson, was sold and never seen again. Handy recalled, 'My own father used to cry in church whenever anyone raised the familiar spiritual, "March Along, I'll See You on the Judgement Day." Once, quite innocently, I asked him the reason for those tears. He answered, "That is what the slaves sang when the white folks sold brother Hanson away."'

Music became the driving force in young W.C. Handy's life. He picked berries, nuts and made lye soap secretly to save enough money to buy a guitar that he'd seen in a shop window. Despite initial resistance from his father, Handy pursued a musical career, studied music and achieved remarkable success. Handy didn't invent the Blues but he did introduce them to the world.

First Recordings

Although the French had pioneered a recording device, Thomas Edison was the first to produce a working model that could record and replay sound and his invention of the phonograph cylinder in 1877 created a sensation and brought him international fame. It also started the phenomenon of recorded music and the recording industry.

George Johnson, born in slavery on a plantation in Virginia, was heard whistling on the Staten Island Ferry – some say by Edison himself – and became the first African-American to be recorded on wax phonograph cylinders, in about 1889, and on disc records in 1895.

Johnson's song, 'Whistling Coon', came from minstrel shows that were notorious for lampooning Africans as ignorant, lazy and superstitious. 'Coon Music' gained wide popularity and by 1890, over six hundred such songs had been published. These bizarre minstrel shows, with performers like Al Jolson, played a powerful role in shaping such stereotypes and popular entertainment continued the propaganda.

The Race to Record the Blues

Perry Bradford was a black vaudeville performer who joined a minstrels' group in New Orleans but ambition took him to New York where he organized a Blues review called 'Made in Harlem' in 1918. After hustling record companies, he reworked James Johnson's 'Mama's and Papa's Blues' as 'Crazy Blues', and in August 1920 persuaded Okeh Records to take a chance and record the song.

'Crazy Blues' made history because it was sung by Mamie Smith, the first black female to record a song with Blues in its title, backed by an all-black band, the Jazz Hounds.

Smith's 'Crazy Blues' was a surprise smash hit and sold a phenomenal seventy-five thousand copies in the month of its release and eventually hit a million. The

✛
The excitement sparked a Blues craze, with fierce rivalry among record companies
✛

excitement sparked a Blues craze, with fierce rivalry among record companies, who raced to find the fastest way to make a hit record. Nine other record companies recorded black female Blues singers in the three years

that followed 'Crazy Blues', and the period was dominated by women like Bessie Smith and Ma Rainey.

Okeh Records' Ralph Peer coined the phrase 'Race
Records' as an industry code for black music intended
for the black market.

The Man who Recorded the Blues: Ralph Peer

Okeh Records aimed at America's immigrant communities ignored by the big labels and they released recordings in German, Czech, Polish, Swedish and Yiddish, but
their success with 'Crazy Blues' alerted Peer to the sales
potential of niche markets and his innovations and discoveries made him a towering figure in the business. He
had a canny knack for recognizing music that people
would buy and had figured out how to make a buck
from the new technology.

Peer was first to record a Blues singer, a twelve-string
guitarist called Ed Andrews, with 'Barrelhouse Blues', in
Atlanta, in April 1924. A year
earlier, he had produced the
first commercial country
recording with Fiddlin' John
Carson's 'Little Old Log
Cabin in the Lane'. Peer virtually started up modern
country music with his discoveries, the Carter Family
and Jimmie Rodgers, and
made up the term 'hillbilly'
to identify such rural music.

✦
Peer was one of the
first to understand the
significance of
copyright and pushed
artists to record new
songs rather than
traditional music
✦

Peer was one of the first to understand the significance of copyright and pushed artists to record new
songs rather than traditional music. The simple reason

was that he only made money from original songs. When he joined the Victor Talking Machine Company (later to become RCA Victor) in 1927, Peer negotiated a phenomenal deal: he would be paid one dollar a year in salary but could take a cut of the royalties for every record sold and every song played on the radio. Backed by Victor's worldwide distribution capabilities, Peer's strategy worked. He pocketed one million dollars a year, at a time when he paid popular artists between $3,000 and $4,000 a year and average annual earnings were about $700.

Peer made early recordings of Louis Armstrong and Fats Waller and virtually every big name in the entertainment industry (Benny Goodman, Bing Crosby, Count Basie, Glenn Miller, etc) covered his songs ('You Are My Sunshine', 'Will the Circle Be Unbroken', 'Georgia on My Mind'). He introduced Latin-tinged music onto the world scene and handled the copyright for most of the popular songs of the age. Today, Peer's business is the largest privately held music publisher in the world. His impact was summarized by one critic's observation: 'The payment of royalties based on authorship and record sales as conceived by Ralph Peer is the basic business model for the entire music industry today.'

Songs owned by Peer continued to hit the charts following the success in 2000 of the Coen Brothers' movie *O Brother Where Art Thou* and the album *Buena Vista Social Club* in 1997, inspired by the Cuban phenomenon the Buena Vista Social Club. But representatives of the Cuban songwriters challenged Peer and in a complex international legal case that lasted seven years, Peer's company failed to wrestle the copyright from the highly successful Buena Vista Social Club. In 2006, a London high court upheld the rights of the Cuban composers, all of whom were dead.

In 1923, Peer pioneered field recordings, an idea other record companies copied; as a result, most of the male Country Blues singers were recorded between 1924 and 1930, at least five years after the success of the classic female Blues singers.

The first Blues superstar was a Texas street singer called Blind Lemon Jefferson, who recorded about one hundred sides. Jefferson was the biggest-selling country Blues singer between 1926 and 1929 and his songs live on. The Beatles recorded 'Matchbox', based on Carl Perkins' version of Jefferson's 'Match Box Blues'. Kurt Cobain picked up a Southern Appalachian traditional song 'Where Did You Sleep Last Night/In the Pines', popularized by Lead Belly, who claimed to have been a guide for Jefferson.

The Radio Takes America By Storm

The good times ended with the news that America's financial infrastructure was collapsing. 24 October 1929 was nicknamed 'Black Thursday' because of panic selling on the New York Stock Exchange and the Wall Street crash led to the era called the Great Depression, putting an end to the prosperity of the 'Roaring Twenties'.

For cheap entertainment, millions turned to the latest technological invention that had recently gained in popularity: the radio. Initially, broadcasters preferred live recordings to recorded music, but things changed in 1935. The kidnapping of Charles Lindberg's baby held the nation spellbound and when Bruno Hauptmann was accused of the crime, everyone relied on the radio for the latest news. During breaks in Hauptmann's trial, DJ Martin Block played recorded music. This innovation proved popular with the growing audience of radio listeners and a trend was launched for recorded music on the radio.

But not everyone was dancing in the aisles.

Copyright Conflict

The American Society of Composers, Authors and Publishers (ASCAP) had been set up in 1914 to license the work of its members and collect royalty payments each time their compositions were played in public. Most of ASCAP's income came from sheet music and live broadcasts, but this changed after radio stations used recorded music and it became ASCAP's largest income source. ASCAP realized the financial potential of the new medium as they watched their income from radio broadcasts leap from $757,450 in 1932 to $5.9 million in 1937.

But many radio broadcasters were convinced that after they purchased a record they had the right to play that music freely and didn't think they should pay an additional royalty fee. ASCAP disagreed.

The conflict reached screaming point as ASCAP declared that if radio stations wanted to play music by the most popular composers of the age (Rodgers and Hart, Cole Porter, George Gershwin, Irving Berlin, etc) they'd have to pay up: ASCAP were doubling their licence fee.

In defiance, the radio stations set up their own rival performing rights organization, Broadcast Music Incorporated (BMI) in 1939, with a lower percentage rate.

If BMI were puzzling over what music they could play on the radio, one man had the answer: Ralph Peer. He had a warehouse full of songs that ASCAP had essentially banned: hillbilly and race music. ASCAP'S monopoly had been broken. The deal put a smile on many faces, including Peer's, as he raced to the bank.

In the past, ASCAP had controlled what music people could listen to and their monopoly gave them the power to shape the nation's musical taste. Since they were the only company in the business, there was no option. While some trained African-American musicians like Harry Burleigh, W.C. Handy and Duke Ellington were included, ASCAP had refused to license most race or country musicians.

While black musicians were responsible for the major innovations in popular music, it was the white imitators who found prominence. Influential black artists were rarely heard on the radio, though there were notable exceptions: such as Duke Ellington's broadcasts from the Cotton Club in Harlem; instead, it was easy for the major networks to ignore black artists and to use white entertainers to cover the popular black music of the time. Most fans didn't know the origins of their favourite songs or styles. Only music registered with ASCAP could be played on the radio.

> ✦
> While black musicians were responsible for the major innovations in popular music, it was the white imitators who found prominence
> ✦

In an article for *Split Images: African-Americans in the Mass Media*, Reebee Garofalo concluded, 'Without this challenge [of BMI to ASCAP] we might never have heard from composers like Huddie Ledbetter, Arthur Big Boy Crudup, Roy Brown, Ivory Joe Hunter, Johnny Otis, Fats Domino and Wynonie Harris.'[46]

Musical Strike

But a new heavyweight contest was around the corner. This time, the powerful musicians' union climbed into the ring with the record industry.

With the huge surge in radio listeners, it was getting easier and cheaper to listen to music. The radio stations cut back on broadcasts with live orchestras, choosing to play recorded music as the cheaper option. When the Wurlitzer Company bought Homer Capehart's Simplex record changing mechanism in 1933, their dazzling juke-box machines used ten-inch vinyl records played at 78 rpm.

The union complained that musicians were losing their jobs because of the new canned music and announced a strike. No new music was recorded after 1 August 1942. The ban was intended to force the record companies to pay royalties for records broadcast on the radio and played on jukeboxes.

Decca Records settled in 1943, but the strike lasted until 1944. When it was over, the musical landscape had changed. The losers were the big bands, as the spotlight switched to smaller combos and crooners such as Bing Crosby and Frank Sinatra.

The Changing System of Listening to Music

In the past, all music was played 'live'. People had to get to where the music was performed in order to hear it. The only way that music could be preserved was for it to be written down. Then it could be passed to other musicians, played, and interpreted by them; it could also be heard by audiences in different places and at different times. The European classical tradition developed in this way. After the composer had written down the music, it was performed by trained musicians.

But music evolved differently in other cultures, and in Africa, the performers and musicians developed varying beats and tempos driven by complex rhythms. One traveller who witnessed the power and glory of African music wrote, 'African rhythm is so complicated that it is exceedingly difficult for a European to analyze it . . . any piece of European music has at any one moment one rhythm in common, a piece of African music always has two or three, sometimes as many as four. From this point of view European music is childishly simple.'

> ✦
> **Radio became a powerful force because it enabled communicators to speak directly to their audience**
> ✦

The main way for people in America to hear music during the late 1940s was live performances – and the radio.

Radio shows were mostly aimed at local audiences so it was unusual for any one artist to reach a national audience. Radio stations identified listener profiles and played music popular with their markets, so individual, local race and country music stations used musicians who played that particular brand of music.

Radio became a powerful force because it enabled communicators to speak directly to their audience.

In 1943, there were only four radio stations in America that played material for a black audience. The problem was that sponsors thought their white audience would turn against them if their programming was linked to blacks and didn't want their products associated with that market.

WDIA in Memphis in 1949 became the first station to use an all-black on-air staff and to play black music all day. Later that year, WERD in Atlanta became the first black-owned station. WERD was located in the same building as the new Southern Christian Leadership Conference, led by Dr Martin Luther King. It's been said that Dr King would hammer on the ceiling of the office with a broomstick as a signal to send the microphone down when he was ready to deliver another public message.

The Memphis radio station created a sensation and in time came to dominate the market.

The major technological advances were adapted for mass audiences and influenced by popular demand. Artists were able to reach audiences way beyond their immediate circle and the medium of radio accelerated that process. With this ability to reach a national audience the stage was set for a cataclysmic musical eruption bustling with innovative and creative ideas and trends. It transcended everyone's imagination and expectation while demonstrating that it was vastly profitable. The genie was wriggling, about to leap out of the bottle . . .

8

Exploiting the Blues

The Blues were described in Martin Scorsese's award-winning documentary, *The Blues: A Musical Journey*, as an American treasure, with no comparable tradition, either in Europe or Africa. Like spirituals – the first original musical form created by the slaves of Africa – this authentically unique roots music had its origins in slavery with influences and echoes from West African rhythms.

The idea of 'African music' is misleading. There isn't any 'African music'. Music varies across the continent and developed differently from European music. In the European tradition, the melody is paramount, enhanced, illuminated by the instruments and the rhythm follows the tune; with West African music, the rhythm is everything, the melody incidental.

Blues covered field hollers, shouts, moans, stomps, ballads, work songs, songs of love and loss, anguish and torment, dance tunes called jump-ups and racy versions called 'hokum'; the songs created mythic black folk heroes of John Henry, Stagger Lee, Dupree; Blues also covered songs of social comment: Blind Blake sang of police brutality ('Police Dog Blues'), and lynchings ('Rope Stretching Blues'). 'Mississippi Boll Weevil Blues' by Charley Patton told of the plague of insects that destroyed many farms in the early 1900s, 'Dry Well Blues' talked of a drought, 'Moon Going Down' spoke of a fire that destroyed a Clarksdale mill. Lonnie Johnson made eight recordings on the theme of floods; Patton's 'High Water Everywhere' and Memphis Minnie's 'When the Levee Breaks' described the flood of 1927; her song was covered by Led Zeppelin in 1970. Doctor Clayton's sarcastic wit could easily fit alongside the best of the 1960s protest singers. His 'Pearl Harbour Blues' recorded three months after the surprise attack by the Japanese navy against the US Naval base in Hawaii on 7 December 1941, told how the Americans sold brass and scrap iron to the Japanese, who turned it into bombs and shells and dropped the explosives on Pearl Harbour 'like rain'.

Blues songs used a twelve-bar structure with a repetition of the first line, a format that remains unchanged to this day.

Blues absorbed the 'call and response' style of the field hollers and the first slave church meetings, with spirituals its strongest influence.

✦
Blues and Gospel music were very close. They had the same origins. They came from the songs of slaves
✦

In an interview with me, Mahalia Jackson, often described as 'the world's greatest Gospel singer', explained, 'Blues and Gospel music were very close. They had the same origins. They came from the songs of slaves. But Blues were songs of despair and Gospel were songs of hope. Blues leave you empty. Makes you feel like you've got nothing left. Gospel shows you a way out of your despair. Tells you not to give up. It was an important lesson for our people. I listened to Blues singers in New Orleans but I vowed I would only sing Gospel. That was my decision.'

Victoria Spivey said the Blues was a 'feeling'. Booker White said it came from the slave fields, 'walking behind a mule way back in slavery time'. Son House remembered singing in the cotton fields as a child, 'Not real singing, just hollerin', but we made up our songs about things that was happening to us at that time and I think that's where the Blues started.' Clint Eastwood said, 'Blues is the only true American art form.' Willie Dixon put it this way, 'The Blues are the roots; everything else is the fruit.' B.B. King affirmed, 'The Blues is the mother of American music. That's what it is – the source.'

Early Blues weren't written down but passed from one musician to another, twisting, evolving, flowing down the Mississippi River, speeding past towns and country, steel rails humming on the Yazoo Delta Railroad or the Yellow Dog, as it was known, played on whatever instruments were available, clapped percussion, distinguished by 'Blue notes', the bending of strings and notes.

Songs in the Folk Tradition

Within the tradition of folk music no one fully owned a song and it was common for Country Blues singers to rework songs and for ideas to flow back and forth between musicians.

The legendary Robert Johnson borrowed lyrically from others, according to author Robert Springer.[47] 'Devil Got My Woman' by Skip James was reworked by Johnson and emerged as 'Hellhound on My Trail'. 'Dust My Broom' carried phrases from three other songs: Carl

Rafferty's 'Mr Carl Blues', Kokomo Arnold's 'Sagefield Woman Blues' and 'Sissy Man Blues;' Johnson turned another Kokomo Arnold song 'Old Original Kokomo Blues' into 'Sweet Home Chicago'. In Johnson's '32–20 Blues', recorded in 1937, six out of the ten stanzas are almost direct copies from '22–20 Blues' by Skip James, recorded six years earlier. James, under the direction of Paramount's Art Laibley, had done much the same. 'How Long Blues' by James in 1931 copied Leroy Carr's 1928 'How Long Blues'.

Sleepy John Estes said he was encouraged to copy the hits of the day but to create a slightly different version of the same song. Chuck Berry, The Rolling Stones, Bob Dylan, John Mayall/Eric Clapton all covered 'It Hurts Me Too' by Elmore James and it is considered one of his songs but the Bluesman got it from Tampa Red's 1949 recording of 'When Things Go Wrong'.

Blind Lemon Jefferson's 'Black Snake Moan' copied Victoria Spivey's 1926 'Black Snake Blues', recorded when she was just sixteen years old. Spivey was apparently annoyed when his version proved more popular but things were quickly resolved between them.

Emerging Styles: Ragtime, Boogie-Woogie

Enslaved Africans recreated the banjo from what they remembered of stringed instruments that they were familiar with in Africa and early forms of the instrument were probably based on the 'akonting', a lute played by the Jola tribe of Senegambia and the 'xalam' of Senegal, which dated back to ancient Egypt. The name 'banjo' was once thought to have originated from the Kimbundu term 'mbanza', though more recently it has been traced to a Senegambian term for the bamboo stick

> ✦
> By the time the Blues evolved and was recorded, the piano and guitar were instruments of choice
> ✦

used for the instrument's neck. Joel Sweeney invented the modern banjo and experts have asserted that it is the only truly American instrument.

'Papa' Charlie Jackson was the first commercially successful 'race' artist who played a banjo strung like a guitar. Jackson's range of ragtime and show songs, in the twenties, included 'Feather Bed', with a phrase that became 'Rock Island Line'.

By the time the Blues evolved and was recorded, the piano and guitar were instruments of choice. The early Country Blues singers were mostly male and favoured the guitar, but they recorded at least five years after the classic female Blues singers, who used the piano and jazz bands as accompaniment.

Analysts direct that these Blues singers changed the idea of popular music from being simple songs that could be easily performed by anyone to works primarily associated with an individual singer. According to Jeff Todd Titon in *The Blues: A Musical Journey*, jazz bands followed singers such as Bessie Smith and 'singers became attached to bands, instead of the reverse'.[48]

Ragtime was a hugely popular craze between 1899 and 1918 and may have been derived from an attempt to use the keyboard to imitate the banjo.

Scott Joplin, the son of a former slave, born about 1868 in Texas, was a piano prodigy whose musical education was funded by his mother's work as a domestic servant. Joplin's rollicking compositions found immediate fame but shocked conservative society at the time, who cited it as evidence of the decadence sweeping the nation. Joplin's rags were revived in the seventies when his composition, 'The Entertainer', was used as the main theme for the Hollywood blockbuster 'The Sting'.

Blind Lemon Jefferson, Blind Blake, Furry Lewis, Mississippi John Hurt and Charley Patton were among the Country Blues musicians who invented and used the finger-picking style of guitar playing by copying the form of Ragtime piano on the strings of the guitar.

Ragtime was followed by the infectious Boogie-woogie piano style that probably originated in the work camps at the start of the twentieth century.

In the Piney Woods in Louisiana, Africans who worked on the railroad gathered in a barrel-house – a tented saloon or shack – to listen to music. As the barrel-house could only afford one musician, piano players developed a style that copied three guitars playing the chords, the melody and the bass. The barrel-house piano players set their tempo to the rhythm of the steam locomotive.

✦

As the barrel-house could only afford one musician, piano players developed a style that copies three guitars playing the chords, the melody and the bass

✦

Clarence Pinetop Smith was the first to use the term on 'Pinetop's Boogie Woogie', recorded in 1928, though there were several musicians playing that style before it took Chicago by storm in the 1930s. Ray Charles modelled himself on Nat King Cole but based his first rhythm song 'Mess Around' on the barrel-house style of Cow Cow Davenport's 'Cow Cow Blues'.

How the Music spread

Africans in the North had integrated into white society and had more opportunities. The first black theatre, the 'African Grove', opened in New York's Greenwich Village in 1821 at the corner of Bleeker Street and Mercer Street.

Storyville was set up in New Orleans in 1897 to contain prostitution in one part of the city and became the red light district. Unable to find work elsewhere, black musicians found New Orleans' red light district became the biggest employer of African-Americans, outside of Broadway. When Storyville was shut down in 1917, musicians like Ferdinand 'Jelly Roll' Morton took off and spread the musical influences of the city.

Morton, like Scott Joplin, was a prolific composer who used the term 'Blues' and 'Jazz' interchangeably, as did record advertisements of the period. At the time, no boundaries between Blues and Jazz existed. Musicians like Louis Armstrong, William Count Basie, Coleman Hawkins, Billie Holliday, now associated with Jazz, were immersed in playing the Blues and Blues singers like Big Joe Turner worked with jazz giants like Count Basie and Edward Duke Ellington. Robert Santelli, the music scholar, confirmed, 'Ellington wrote compositions and arrangements that were steeped in the Blues.'[49]

In 1921, W.C. Handy's partner, Harry Pace, started his own label 'Pace Phonograph Company' (later 'Black Swan Records') but sold its catalogue to Paramount in 1924. It was the first label to be owned, controlled by and marketed to African-Americans.

The first exodus of African-Americans from the Southern states occurred during World War I as factories in the North needed male workers since their youth had joined the armed services. Again, in 1940, huge numbers of blacks left the South for Northern cities seeking work in war factories. Santelli noted that about nearly three million blacks moved North between 1940 and 1960, making the migration one of the largest shifts of people in twentieth-century America.

As Africans moved from the South, numerous styles of music evolved. According to *The Blues: A Musical Journey*, Blues in Texas sounded relaxed and upbeat, New Orleans was brassy, Memphis vaudeville-influenced, the Mississippi Delta raw and passionate, and in Chicago, it turned electric.

On the West coast, Aaron Thibeaux (T-Bone) Walker invented the modern guitar style and developed a solo type of playing that was used by Riley Blues Boy King, Chuck Berry and virtually everyone that followed. Walker's acrobatic stunts proved popular on tour. Everyone wanted to see him play the guitar behind his back while doing the splits or to watch him work the frets with his teeth. Johnny Guitar

✦

As Africans moved from the South, numerous styles of music evolved

✦

Watson copied Walker by playing with his teeth while doing a handstand. Jimi Hendrix's guitar antics stunned cinema audiences in 'Woodstock', but, like most things, it had been tried before.

The Country Blues of the Mississippi Delta have come to be viewed as 'the land where the Blues began' but, in *In Search of the Blues*[50] Marybeth Hamilton argued that this notion was invented in the mid-1940s by an elite group – a 'Blues mafia' – led by James McKune, who were seeking for a voice that matched their opinion of what the Blues should sound like. After they discovered old 78 rpm recordings that revealed the searing, haunting music of Charley Patton, Son House and Robert Johnson, the legend of the Country Blues was hit on; Country Blues became the cornerstone of the premise and the power and impact of these scratchy old recordings took hold.

The music of Patton, House and Johnson inspired Muddy Waters and he became the most important link between the acoustic sounds of the Delta and the amplified, hard driving Blues from urban Chicago.

Waters, born McKinley Morganfield, picked cotton for fifty cents a day on the Stovall Plantation in Clarksdale, Mississippi and learned directly from performers such as Son House. In 1943, he took a train to Chicago and recorded several classics for Chess Records. Although his chart success ended in 1956, Waters became a hugely influential artist and his 1950's song 'Rollin' Stone' inspired the title of a Rock magazine and an English band.

Jimmy Reed followed Waters and moved from Mississippi to Chicago in 1948. He transposed the boogie-woogie beat to the harmonica and to the guitar and used his bass player, Eddie Taylor, to copy the left hand of the pianists.

Chicago became a nerve centre for Blues performers like Muddy Waters, Chester 'Howling Wolf' Burnett, and John Lee Hooker, who lit a torch for the Blues revival that would sweep the musical world in the 1960s.

Jump Blues

Louis Jordan's sleek swing combo picked up on the Boogie-woogie craze and he became the pivotal connection between the end of the big band period and the new music that emerged from the African community. Jordan's 'Jump Blues' ruled the hit parade after the war with an astonishing fifty-seven hits on the Rhythm & Blues charts, with eighteen Number Ones. From 1941 to 1952, he was the undisputed 'King of the Juke Box' and Ray Charles, Little Richard and Chuck Berry have all acknowledged his influence on their music. Piero Scaruffi commented, 'Few people noticed it, but Carl Hogan played a powerful guitar riff on Jordan's "Ain't that just like a woman" in 1946 that, ten years later, would make Chuck Berry's fortune.'[51]

Like Jordan, others such as Erskine Hawkins, crossed the border between Blues and Jazz with songs like 'Tuxedo Junction' in 1939. Big Joe Turner worked with Count Basie and Duke Ellington, among others, songs such as 'Shake Rattle and Roll' made him a huge star of the era. Wynonie Harris and Amos Milburn used the same jump rhythm formula to produce popular hits and these musicians (with others like Roy Brown) became key figures who set the template for the revolution that was to follow.

From Race to Rhythm & Blues

Jerry Wexler, a reporter on *Billboard* magazine, called these new sounds 'Rhythm & Blues' (R&B) and the industry used it as a marketing term for black music. Wexler later produced numerous classic R&B songs including 'What'd I Say' for Ray Charles and several decades later, 'Slow Train Coming' for Bob Dylan.

In search of a better life, millions of freed slaves and their descendants left the South in the 1940s for cities of the North; Chicago's African-American population increased by 77 per cent and it became the second black city after New York's Harlem. They suddenly appeared as recognizable consumers on the Big Business's radar.

Popular music, like every part of American life – public water fountains, restaurants, toilets, transport, housing – was segregated. Record companies advertised exclusively to African-Americans and the products were sold only in black outlets. The Race Records Charts had been set up in 1942 and renamed the Harlem Hit Parade three years later; in 1949 it became the R&B charts.

At the time, the music industry was controlled by six companies: Columbia, Victor, Decca, Capital, MGM and Mercury. The major record companies created labels aimed specifically for black performers (RCA's Blackbird, Capitol's Black & White and Columbia's Okeh) and they established separate categories for pop, Country & Western, with 'race' for black music. But they had little interest in the race market and this enabled smaller independent labels to set up in business; one estimate has it that over four hundred labels had emerged by the end of 1949.

> ✦
> **Popular music, like every part of American life – public water fountains, restaurants, toilets, transport, housing – was segregated**
> ✦

All the early R&B hits came from the independent labels (Imperial, Modern, Speciality, Atlantic) and featured artists (including Antoine Fats Domino's 'The Fat Man', Ike Turner/Jackie Brenston's 'Rocket 88', Lloyd Price's 'Lawdy Miss Clawdy', and Big Joe Turner's 'Chains of Love') who would influence the next earthquake in popular music that was about to sweep the world.

Exploiting the Blues

The music business, like any other, is driven by the demand for profits. Recorded music and radio broadcasts had changed the role of music from a live local event that demanded involvement from its audience into a product created by someone, remotely connected, who decided what commodity would be produced for passive consumers, with the incentive of financial profit for key participants who controlled the gateway.

The hidden history of modern music has a dark side that cannot conceal the often-ruthless exploitation of black artists and the cold prejudice that overshadowed the culture of the time.

Rural Blues musicians were unaware of how the royalty system operated and few registered with the Copyright Office. According to Robert Springer, 'The recording industry very rarely conceded royalties to black artists.' Most of the copyright for Blues (and country) music was undertaken by music publishers working with the record companies.

From 1924, Paramount's Mayo Williams registered about a hundred Blues compositions a year, over a five-year period. Williams was the most successful black producer of race records and probably the only one operating at that level. He was accused of following the custom of the time by avoiding paying royalties to artists if he could. From 1928 to 1932, through his State Street Music, Williams registered five hundred songs. Ralph Peer registered an astounding 3,500 songs, all originals or arrangements, via Southern Music Corporation.

Obviously, entrepreneurs in the music business could increase their profits by dodging paying royalties; they found that black musicians were easy targets who could

✦

Blues artists were paid a flat performance fee for recordings, handed out after each session

✦

be exploited without a contract or persuaded to sign away their rights.

Blues artists were paid a flat performance fee for recordings, handed out after each session. Country Blues singers received between $20–$50 per side; some were paid with a bottle of whisky, though Ralph Peer allegedly said that some would do it for free.

- Columbia paid Bessie Smith $125 for each usable side, according to Robert Springer. Her pianist, acting as her manager, pocketed half that fee. When her husband discovered – and ended – this arrangement, her fee went up to $200 per side. She was persuaded to sign an exclusive contract, though the royalty clause was struck from the document and she was unaware of its significance. Springer insisted that Bessie Smith 'single-handedly' provided jobs for many at Columbia. He's probably right. She was the best-selling Blues singer of her time.

- Lightnin' Hopkins settled for a one-off, cash-per-tune sum with no royalty payment of any kind.

- Jimmy Witherspoon recorded 'Ain't Nobody's Business', a big hit on the Supreme label, owned by Al Patrick. He said, 'I didn't get one penny royalty. Patrick paid me a flat fee for the session. I was supposed to get so much on each record sold, which he never paid me.'

- Saul Bihari, founder of Modern, explained how the recording sessions went: 'We used to bring 'em in, give 'em a little bottle of booze and say, 'Sing me a song about your girl.' Or, 'Sing me a song about Christmas.' They'd pluck around a little on their guitars, then say 'OK', and make up a song as they went along. We'd give them a subject and off they'd go. When it was time to quit, we'd give them a wave that they had ten seconds to finish.'

- A Columbia representative tried to make a deal with Ahmet Ertegun, president of Atlantic Records, for distribution rights to the successful race records from Ertegun's label. When the Columbia agent heard that Atlantic were paying their artists more than three percent he was truly shocked. He told Ertegun, '"You're paying those people royalties? You must be out of your mind!" Of course he didn't call them "people". He called them something else.'

- In *Heart and Soul*, the authors declared, 'Legend has it that Gee Records rewarded [Frankie] Lymon's efforts on the group's first top ten hit, "Why Do Fools Fall in Love?" with a hot dog purchased from a street vendor.'[52]

- Alan Lomax recorded Son House for the Library of Congress in 1941. In *The Blues: A Musical Journey*, Christopher John Farley revealed how the Blues man was paid, 'House was given a cold Coca-Cola for his work.' Son House's recordings (six to ten songs for Paramount in 1930 and nineteen songs for Lomax in 1941 and 1942) were discovered decades later and established his role in defining the Blues. The White Stripes dedicated their self-titled first album to House, covered his 'Death Letter', and Jack White performed the song at the 2004 Grammy Awards.

Springer noted that the original contracts Blues singers signed were often limited to the medium at the time, i.e. phonograph or vinyl records; foreign rights were frequently forgotten or ignored. The Rhythm & Blues Foundation based in Philadelphia argued that these contracts were used when their material was reissued on CD, thus ignoring any further royalty payments.

✦

The 1909 copyright law allowed authors to copyright the original sheet music

✦

tracts were used when their material was reissued on CD, thus ignoring any further royalty payments.

The 1909 copyright law allowed authors to copyright the original sheet music; it wasn't possible to copyright a specific recording of a song. Since royalties are paid to writers and publishers and not to the performer, there is a financial incentive to record many versions of the same song. As a result, songs had an R&B version alongside a Country & Western (C&W) version.

- In 1949, Johnny Wills (Bob's brother) had a smash hit with 'Rag Mop'. It became a signature song for the Ames Brothers; Lionel Hampton and Joe Liggins covered it for the race market. Wills named himself co-composer. However, when challenged with a lawsuit, he acknowledged that he hadn't written a note, but insisted that his steel guitarist, Deacon Anderson, had written it all. Wills and Anderson lost the case. The mystery is solved when you listen to Henry Red Allen's 'Get the Mop'. It's the same song.

- 'Rockin' with Red' by William Piano Red Perryman had several C&W copies with titles such as 'Rock Me' by Lucky Joe Almond and 'She Sure Can Rock Me' by Roy Hall.

- King Records cut both a C&W and pop version of 'Sixty Minute Man' in addition to the R&B original by Billy Ward and the Dominoes on Federal, its subsidiary label.

If songs looked like being a hit, competitors would rush out an alternative and, with better distribution and marketing, they could catch quick sales while wiping out the original.

- Woolworths had its own label (Embassy) dedicated to cheap copies of popular tunes. Inevitably, black artists with the smaller independent labels saw their songs covered by white artists from the bigger companies. With better distribution and marketing, they easily outsold the original and reached the growing demand for R&B music that was increasing in popularity amongst both black and white audiences. In the process, numerous black musicians were victims of exploitation: Don Mclean called the cover versions a 'racist tool'.

- LaVern Baker was infuriated with the exact imitation of her songs and arrangements by white vocalist, Georgia Gibbs, whose cover versions outsold the original. In exasperation, Baker took her case to the U.S. Congress but they could only confirm that it was impossible to copyright a particular arrangement of a song.

- In 1942, Peggy Lee heard Lil Green's version of 'Why Don't You Do Right?' and, with a little help from Benny Goodman, she turned it into a hit that brought her to prominence. Green's song was taken from 'Weed Smoker's Dream' by Memphis Minnie.

- The Prisonaires recorded 'Just Walking in the Rain' and the song hit the R&B top ten in 1953. The five-member group were all serving life sentences at the Tennessee State Prison and recorded in chains, under armed guard at Sun Studios in Memphis. The song had been written by Johnny Bragg, the leader of the group, who claimed to have been wrongfully imprisoned. In his biography, *Just Walking in the Rain*, published in 2001, Bragg revealed that the publishing credit went to Red Wortham as part of the recording deal, who allegedly sold it to Gene Autry. The book stated that fifteen years later, 'Wortham admitted he was not only receiving publishing and writing royalties, but he was also getting the group's artist royalties from Sun.' Three years after the Prisonaires version, the song was a smash pop hit for Johnny Ray.[53]

> ⟡
>
> **The Prisonaires record 'Just Walking in the Rain' and the song hit the R&B top ten in 1953**
>
> ⟡

- Pat Boone had numerous hit singles with covers and his label, Dot, was the most successful at the practice, Reebee Garofalo reported. Boone copied Little Richard's first hit 'Tutti Frutti' and took his cover version into the pop charts leaving the original far behind.

When I asked Little Richard (real name Richard Penniman) about Boone's covers, he reacted with a raucous whoop. 'Whoooeee! Oh Lawdy!' he exclaimed, clasped his palms heavenward and rolled his eyes.

He told me, 'Pat Boone! I was so frustrated that my song "Tutti Frutti" had been covered in that way that I planned my revenge. I decided to write and sing a song so fast with a tongue twister that he would never be able to copy. That's why I wrote "Long Tall Sally". I said, no one but me would be able to sing this song.'

In his luxury suite at London's Hilton Hotel, he broke into a spontaneous version of the song, taking the lyrics at breakneck speed. Hearing his famous 'Ooooh!' close up was intoxicating.

Richard was both right and wrong. No one could sing it. But they tried, including Pat Boone.

Little Richard's flamboyant, rollicking version of 'Long Tall Sally' hit No. 1 in the R&B charts and stayed at the top for six weeks. Pat Boone did copy it but could only manage No. 8 on the pop charts.

The night I interviewed Little Richard, the tabloids had splashed the revelation that Mick Jagger had been forced to return a one million dollar advance for a tell-all book about his life. Jagger couldn't remember the past. After I handed him a copy of the paper, Richard paced the room and appeared both outraged and frantic. 'He had to give one million dollars back! Mick can't remember!' He kept repeating the sentence. After absorbing the news, he became pensive. 'They gave Mick Jagger one million dollars for his story. They would never give us black folk that kind of money.' He then went through a list of black artists who had been ripped off, lost money or died penniless.

- Sylvester Weaver made the first solo country Blues recordings in 1923 released by Ralph Peer on Okeh Records. He used a knife on his guitar in a similar style to the anonymous musician that W.C. Handy had heard in Tutwiler in 1903. Weaver died virtually forgotten in 1960; four decades later, in 1992, his grave finally acquired a headstone, arranged by the

Kentuckiana Blues Society. Yet, his music lives on. His second recording, 'Guitar Rag', played on a guitar-banjo, in 1923, was 'adapted' by the talented Leon McAuliffe and became a country standard for Bob Willis and the Texas Playboys. They called it 'Steel Guitar Rag'.

- Canned Heat's raw earthy Blues featured prominently in 'Woodstock' but their songs were borrowed from Willie Brown ('Future Blues'), William Harris ('Bullfrog Blues') and Blind Willie McTell ('Statesboro Blues'). Robert Springer concluded that the California-based band exploited these songs: 'cashing in thousands of dollars in royalties that, to say the least, they did not entirely deserve.'

✦

Led Zeppelin's first hit single 'Whole Lotta Love' and 'Bring It On Home' from their second album were 'borrowed' from Willie Dixon

✦

- Springer explained how the Rolling Stones were able to appropriate Robert Johnson's 'Love in Vain' on their *Let it Bleed* album; Johnson had recorded the classic in 1937 but hadn't registered its copyright. The Stones' record company contested the case but their argument was dismissed and the court upheld Johnson's right of ownership.

- Led Zeppelin's first hit single 'Whole Lotta Love' and 'Bring it on Home' from their second album were 'borrowed' from Willie Dixon, whose record company's publishing arm, Arc, successfully sued the British group. But Arc never told Dixon and he had to personally sue the company and later Led

Zeppelin, before he earned any money from either song.

The Library of Congress created the privately funded Archive of American Folk Song in 1928 but the project lay dormant during the Great Depression. It was taken up by John Lomax, who bought a sound recorder from Thomas Edison's widow and set off in 1933 on an extensive series of excursions with his son, Alan, to catalogue songs for the Library. Edison's bulky recording device occupied the trunk and much of the back seat of their sedan. The recorder measured two feet square and a foot tall, weighed three hundred pounds and required two car batteries to power its large amplifier.

Lomax was not the first to record rural musicians. Marybeth Hamilton's *In Search of the Blues* noted that Howard Odum, a Georgia-born sociologist, may have been the first person to record the Blues in Lafayette County, forty miles east of the Mississippi Delta in 1907.[54] Odum heard musicians singing songs made up of a single line, repeated two or three times. Caspar Smith, editor of the *Observer Music Monthly* said that Odum perceived himself as a scientist with his phonograph an instrument of science. 'It was insight into the potential of the "Negro race" that he really sought.' Odum captured the Blues in their purest form but the cylinders that they were recorded on were lost or discarded in 1920. In that same year Dorothy Scarborough, a teacher and grandchild of slave-owners, travelled the South in pursuit of music that would confirm the Negro's 'highest gift, his spontaneity'. She believed some of the music of black Southerners reflected 'the lighter, happier side of slavery'.

The recordings made by the Lomaxes were hugely significant in preserving the past and their tens of thousands of recordings from across the US, Europe, the United Kingdom and the Caribbean are to be released on a comprehensive 150-CD collection. These historic recordings include early performances by Woody Guthrie, Pete Seeger, Son House, Muddy Waters, Jelly Roll Morton, Burl Ives and numerous others.

It was at Angola State Prison that the Lomaxes made one of their greatest discoveries when they recorded Huddie Ledbetter, better known as Lead Belly. Following his release from prison, the Lomaxes organized a tour for Lead Belly and he created a sensation with his wide collection of songs that included 'The Midnight Special', 'Cottonfields', 'Rock Island Line' and 'Goodnight Irene', a No. 1 hit for Pete Seeger's group, the Weavers.

The Lomaxes played a critical role in the emergence of rural music but their reputation has been tarnished by reports of their treatment of Lead Belly and others.

In *Dead, But Still Stealing*, Dave Marsh, a former editor at *Rolling Stone*, observed that to all concerned, the Lomaxes 'wrote' songs such as 'Stagolee', 'John Henry', took credit for 'Tom Dooley' and several classic spirituals, including 'O Freedom'. Marsh concluded that for such theft they deserved the 'Nobel Prize for Gall'.[55]

- 'Goodnight Irene' named Lead Belly and John Lomax as the authors of the song, according to John Pareles and the profits from such recordings supported the Lomaxes international song-collecting trips in the 1950s. They named themselves as co-authors of songs they recorded as if they had written the songs themselves, splitting royalties, a system that was in place at the time and widely used by commercial record producers and publishers of the period.

- Lomax recorded Muddy Waters in 1941 and 1942 but Robert Gordon's biography of the great Blues singer, *Can't Be Satisfied*, claimed that Lomax never paid the $20 promised for the recording.

- In 2002, a former inmate in the Mississippi State Penitentiary named James Carter was astonished to receive a cheque for $20,000. It was his portion of the royalties for 'Po Lazarus', the song played over the opening credits for the Coen Brothers' hit film, *O Brother, Where Art Thou*? The recording had been made in 1959 and included in the film soundtrack that had outsold Michael Jackson and Mariah Carey in 2002. It had taken forty-three years for Carter to receive any money for the song.

> ✦
> It was his portion of the royalties for 'Po Lazarus', the song played over the oppening credits for the Coen Brothers' hit film, *O Brother, Where Art Thou*?
> ✦

- Alan Lomax passed on a South African song called 'Mbube' (Zulu for 'lion') to Pete Seeger who was taken with the catchy melody. He re-titled it 'Wimoweh' and his version, with the Weavers, hit the top twenty in 1952. The infectious melody hit the top again as 'The Lion Sleeps Tonight' in the 1960s and since then it has been covered by over 150 artists (including Jimmy Dorsey, Ladysmith Black Mambazo, Brian Eno, REM, NSYNC and the 1985 England World Cup Soccer Squad) and used in fifteen feature films including *Coming to America, Ace Ventura: Pet Detective* and the Disney hit *The Lion King*. It was estimated to have made $15million from *The Lion King* alone. Yet, tragically, the song's original author died penniless in 1962 and had to wait eighteen years for a headstone on his grave.

South African journalist Rian Malan uncovered the story in *Rolling Stone* magazine in 2000. Seeger copyrighted 'Wimoweh' in the name of the group, the Weavers, while George David Weiss, co-author of 'Can't Help Falling in Love', tinkered with the melody, rewrote some lyrics, claimed authorship of 'The Lion Sleeps Tonight', and, according to Malan, has received publishing royalties ever since.[56]

'Mbube' was written in 1939 by Solomon Linda but the Zulu musician only received a flat fee for the recording, reportedly less than a dollar. Under British copyright law, in effect at the time, the rights should have reverted to his heirs twenty-five years after his death, in 1962. Pete Seeger acknowledged the true author of the song, but Disney fought the lawsuit brought by Linda's family, eventually settling in 2006.

> ✦
> 'Mbubu' was written in 1939 by Solomon Linda but the Zulu musician only received a flat fee for the recording, reportedly less than a dollar
> ✦

- Muddy Waters directed Chuck Berry to Chess Records but they thought he was a black hillbilly singer and suggested that his music needed a bigger beat. Berry beefed up his original demo and 'Ida Red' (a traditional country standard) became 'Maybellene'. Chess persuaded the powerful DJ Alan Freed to give it a spin on his radio show. Freed was an influential figure in the music industry and, for his part in the song's success, he picked up a portion of the writer's credit. With radio exposure 'Maybellene' was a run-away success. Everyone was happy except for Berry when he studied his royalty statement and learned that money had been deducted and paid to Freed for the song he hadn't written. For Berry, it was a crash course in business. Sometime later, he sued the Beach Boys. Their first hit 'Surfin' USA' sounded too close to his own 'Sweet Little Sixteen'. Berry won.

Not everyone acted dishonourably. Eric Clapton acknowledged Robert Johnson as the author of 'From Four Until Late', even though he didn't need to, since Johnson hadn't registered the song's copyright.

Fats Domino used his success to insist that his recording deals had regular royalty payments instead of the single payment contract that was handed out to others. Ivory Joe Hunter was one of the first black artists to set up his own label, first Ivory and then in 1942, Pacific Records.

9

How Slave Music Rocked the World

Memphis was called the murder capital of America in the 1900s, yet it had more churches than service stations. It was Memphis that banned *Annie Get Your Gun* because it featured a black railway conductor among its characters.

After the Civil War, many former slaves left the rural areas and headed for cities like Memphis, searching for their families and trying to make a better life. Stanley Booth reported 'there were only four thousand Negroes in Memphis in 1860 but by 1870 there were fifteen thousand'.

Memphis' notorious Beale Street was described by newspaperman Gilmore Millen as a street of 'business and love and murder and theft', where:

> merchants, pawnbrokers, country Negroes from plantations, Creole prostitutes, painted fag men, sleepy gamblers, slick young chauffeurs, crooks, bootleggers, dope peddlers, rich property owners, powdered women, labour agents, blind musicians, confidence men, hardworking Negroes from sawmills and cotton warehouses and factories and stores meet and stand on street corners, slip upstairs to gambling joints, rooming hotels, barber shops, bawdy houses.[57]

Memphis was also the location for the most powerful black radio station WDIA where B.B. King worked as a disc jockey.

With many technological advances, including versatile hardware and the introduction of magnetic tape, an invention developed by the Nazis during World War II, it became easier to produce recordings and, in 1950, Sam Philips opened the Memphis Recording Service on 706 Union Avenue in Memphis. Philips recorded local musicians like B.B. King, Chester 'Howling Wolf' Burnett, Herman 'Junior' Parker and then sold or leased the masters to larger record companies. Two years later he scraped together the finances to launch Sun Records.

✦

The thunder and excitement of the R&B beat had created its own imitators

✦

The thunder and excitement of the R&B beat had created its own imitators. The problem was that the covers lacked the power of the original but because of its segregated society, mainstream white America only heard the copies. Sam Philips repeatedly told his assistant, Marion Keisker, 'If I could find a white man who had the Negro sound and the Negro feel, I could make a billion dollars.'

Walking in Memphis, Elvis Presley had grown up poor and was immersed in black culture, particularly the music, both secular and sacred. He didn't have to travel to get to the Memphis ghetto. He lived in it.

Philips decided to give Elvis a chance in the studio but none of the standards and crooning country ballads that they tried out seemed any good. During a break in the session, Elvis pulled out a spontaneous version of an old Blues song from 1946 by Arthur Big Boy Crudup called 'That's All Right Mama'. The nineteen-year-old's version followed the original closely but it carried a distinctive authenticity. Scorsese's *The Blues: A Musical Journey* declared Elvis sang 'it like no one had ever sung a Blues song before'.

Philips took an acetate of the recording to the local radio station's *Red Hot & Blue* programme, known for playing race music and R&B. The DJ, Dewey Phillips, was careful to mention that the singer had attended Humes High School. It was a signal to the listeners that the musician was white. The music sounded black.

Philips had found his white man who could sing the Blues.

The Origins of Rock & Roll

Little Richard has a swing even when he talks. He was direct. Point blank. He told me, 'Elvis opened the door for black singers and black musicians to come charging through. We were able to "crossover" into the mainstream, to get established quicker. Make more money. Things became easier. There were a lot of people playing that kind of music but Elvis was the one that turned everyone on to the music that black people were playing. He turned on America. He took us to a different place. Everything was different after Elvis.'

Everything was different. But not everyone knew how to categorize the new music. Elvis's first six singles for Sun Records were out-there R&B, yet he registered on the C&W

> ✦
>
> There were a lot of people playing that kind of music but Elvis was the one that turned everyone on to the music that black people were playing
>
> ✦

charts. He performed for the Grand Ole Opry in Nashville but was apparently told not to give up his day job as a truck driver. Country music promoter Tillman Franks booked Presley's first appearance on the Louisiana Hayride on 16 October 1954, without ever seeing him in person but referred to him as 'that new black singer with the funny name'. R&B and Country flowed back and forth. Even popular country singer Marty Robbins recorded a version of 'That's All Right Mama' that outsold Elvis.

Elvis was called the Memphis Flash, King of Western Bop, Hillbilly Cat. He was not yet the King of Rock & Roll.

The words 'Rock & Roll' were first used in 'The Camp Meeting Jubilee' by an unknown Gospel quartet in 1916, while Trixie Smith recorded 'My Man Rocks Me (With One Steady Roll)' in 1922. Wild Bill Moore's 'Rock and Roll' in 1949 came two years after Roy Brown's 'Good Rocking Tonight', the first to feature a backbeat, with an even wilder version by Wynonie Harris.

Although the words 'Rock & Roll' weren't used, Rock's recognizable sounds could be heard on 'Tiger Rag' by the Washboard Rhythm Kings in 1931. 'Flying Home' by Lionel Hampton and his orchestra in 1939 showcased a tenor sax solo by Illinois Jacquet that was recreated and refined live by Arnett Cobb; the emotional, honking sax became a model for Rock & Roll solos after that.

Alan Freed's radio show in Cleveland played the original hits (not the covers) of Louis Jordan, Wynonie Harris, Amos Milburn, Roy Brown, Fats Domino, all familiar names on the R&B charts. Except, Freed called the music Rock & Roll. It was 1951.

In black culture, Rock & Roll was just another name for R&B and everyone recognized the familiar signals of boogie-woogie piano, honking sax, rocking bass. Fats Domino expressed it succinctly. He said, 'I don't know the difference between Rock & Roll and R&B.'

The First Rock & Roll Record

In 1951, the fastest car on the road was the Oldsmobile 88 with the Rocket V8 engine provided as standard equipment. The car inspired Ike Turner to write 'Rocket 88', similar to 'Cadillac Boogie' by Jimmy Liggins. Turner recorded 'Rocket 88' at Sam Philips's Memphis Recording Studio, with his band, the Rhythm Kings, featuring Jackie Brenston on saxophone and vocals, and each member was paid a flat fee of $20 for the session. Philips sold the master tape to Chess Records in Chicago. When the record was released the label stated that it was performed by 'Jackie Brenston and his Delta Cats', and songwriting credit went to Brenston. Four weeks later it was Number One.

Today, 'Rocket 88' has been hailed as the first Rock & Roll record while others have argued that this accolade should go to Bill Haley's 'Rock Around the Clock'. *Rolling Stone* magazine took the controversial step of bestowing the title on Elvis's 'That's All Right Mama'. Both Haley's and Presley's recordings were made in 1954.

Meanwhile, Blues enthusiast Morgan Wright emphasized that 'Rocket 88', from 1951, was a typical R&B number of its day, with little difference between the Turner/Brenston song and the music played at the time by Fats Domino, Big Joe Turner, Arthur Big Boy Crudup, Wynonie Harris and others.[58]

Wright explained that Roy Brown was an unknown who had offered the Jump Blues 'Good Rocking Tonight' to Wynonie Harris, an established star, who turned it down in 1947. After Brown's version hit the charts, Harris covered the song the same year but it was released in 1948. Brown's original had a slow rocking shuffle Blues beat but Harris changed the rhythm to an up-tempo Gospel beat with hand clapping on the back beat, sounding like Black Gospel music of the time. Wright holds that it was the sound of Rock & Roll bursting out. From this point on, several musicians copied the rhythm and Wright contended that at least fifty different records could meet the challenge for the first Rock & Roll record including: Louis Jordan's 'Saturday Night Fish Fry'; Fats Domino's 'The Fat Man'; Jimmy Preston's 'Rock the Joint'; Roy Brown's 'Rocking at Midnight'; Wild Bill Moore's 'Rock and Roll'; Goree Carter's 'Rock Awhile'; Will Bradley's 'Down the Road A Piece'; Big Joe Turner's 'Shake Rattle and Roll'; Hank Ballard and the Midnighters's 'Work With Me Annie'; Billy Ward and his Dominoes' 'Have Mercy Baby'; Cecil Gant's 'We're Gonna Rock' or Muddy Waters's 'I'm Your Hoochie Coochie Man'.

✦

Despite his influential role in shaping the emerging new music, Brown remained in relative obscurity

✦

Wright named Roy Brown as the founding father of Rock & Roll. 'Roy Brown took all the pieces of the puzzle and put them together into the first full-blown rock and roll.' Despite his influential role in shaping the emerging new music, Brown remained in relative obscurity and was unable to benefit from the music he helped to invent. He spent much of his life as a door-to-door encyclopaedia salesman.

Ten years before anyone had seen Jerry Lee Lewis kick away the piano stool, stand upright and hammer the keyboards, Harry 'the Hipster' Gibson had done it all before. He was the first white musician to play in a Rock & Roll style. Dressed in a zoot suit, popular fashion in Harlem's hip Jazz culture, he copied their jive slang and the rocking piano boogie style; even rare video clips make it hard to comprehend that such vintage recordings were filmed in the forties. Gibson learned from Fats Waller and played in Harlem as a teenager, but his outrageous songs, like 'Who Put the Benzedrine in Mrs. Murphy's Ovaltine', meant he was deemed too risqué and he was blacklisted by the music industry.

Bill Haley and the Comets were a C&W band that recorded covers of R&B songs, though his record label, Decca, described 'Crazy Man Crazy' as a fox trot. Haley saw a black group called the Treniers in the early 1950s and in 2001, Claude Trenier told an interviewer, 'We knew Bill Haley when he was a Country & Western band. We were playing Riptide in Wildwood, New Jersey in the summer of 1950. He was playing across the street. He said, "Man, I like what you are doing."' Was Haley influenced by the encounter or did he copy their style? He recorded 'Rock Around the Clock' in 1954 but it only took off when it was featured in the Hollywood film *The Blackboard Jungle* in 1955. The song itself is remarkably similar to Hank Williams's 'Move It on Over', which in turn resembled Charley Patton's 'Going to Move to Alabama', partly derived from Jim Jackson's 'Kansas City Blues', from 1927.

The Big Bang of Rock & Roll

For white mainstream America, the electric shock came when Elvis Presley was seen on national television and his music ushered R&B into unsuspecting white American homes nationwide in 1956.

The popular songs of the age were bland ballads such as Mitch Miller's 'Yellow Rose of Texas'; the Four Aces' 'Love is a Many Splendid Thing'; Roger Williams' 'Autumn Leaves'; Tennessee Ernie Ford's 'Sixteen Tons' and Dean Martin's 'Memories Are Made of This'.

Suddenly, Elvis, along with Chuck Berry, Little Richard, Jerry Lee Lewis, etc were seen as inventing a new musical form that took the name of Rock & Roll. They became the brand of Rock & Roll.

Ironically, while Chuck Berry and Little Richard will always be at the top of any roots-of-Rock & Roll list, Ike Turner has rarely been associated with this line-up. At the time he was marketed as an R&B artist.

The lines were blurred. *Rock 'N' Roll Revue* was a feature film released in movie theatres around the country in 1955 and featured Duke Ellington and Nat King Cole, among others.

But the idea that Rock emerged from a 'big bang' explosion was challenged by Blues aficionado Morgan Wright, who said, 'When you read most books on the origin of Rock & Roll, they describe an explosion that hit around 1954 or '55. All of a sudden, Elvis, Bill Haley, Chuck Berry, Little Richard and others were playing perfectly developed Rock & Roll, as if it came out of nowhere. Some portray it as a magical moment in a recording studio, with musicians goofing around during a break and playing some unrehearsed jam and somehow accidentally inventing a whole new type of music. Ridiculous.'

Little Richard's recordings, such as the Jump Blues styled 'Get Rich Quick' prior to September 1955's 'Tutti Frutti' were similar to other songs out at the time and weren't big hits. Harry Gibson was the first white musician playing Boogie Rock whose performances seemed remarkably similar to Jerry Lee Lewis, except the recordings were at least ten years earlier. And numerous boogie-woogie pianists like Cecil Gant pioneered the music that Lewis would recreate and popularize establishing his place amongst the pioneers of Rock.

Chuck Berry didn't record till May 1955 but he was a brilliant lyricist, with several classic songs that secured his reputation as Rock & Roll royalty. Johnnie Johnson played piano on virtually every early recording and later charged that the compositions were created by Berry and Johnson as a team. The subsequent lawsuit was thrown out of court in 2002. But Berry's influences aren't that hard to spot. Fred Rothwell, author of *Chuck Berry's Recorded Legacy* pointed out that Berry's guitar introduction to 'Johnny B Goode' was taken virtually note for note from Louis Jordan's 'Ain't That Just Like a Woman'.[59] Rothwell wryly commented, 'No wonder Chuck always mentions Carl Hogan when asked about his favourite guitarists.' Rothwell stated that Berry picked up ideas from T-Bone Walker's 'I Got a Break, Baby' from 1942 and Big Joe Turner's 'Around the Clock Blues' inspired 'Reeling and Rocking'. Luther Allison said that he saw J.B. Lenoir do a duck walk on stage before Chuck Berry. Berry himself has acknowledged that his major influences were Louis Jordan, T-Bone Walker and Nat King Cole.

> ✦
> Chuck Berry didn't record till May 1955 but he was a brilliant lyricist
> ✦

Elvis didn't 'go' anywhere to absorb the rhythms of Memphis. The Presleys were poor whites who lived amongst the black communities in Memphis. He was there. Young Elvis attended the Gospel shows, but also knew the clubs and juke joints downtown. He was in the audience at Roy Brown's concerts and at the clubs listening to B.B. King. Both remember him. He was probably in the studio when Johnny Bragg and the Prisonaires recorded 'Just Walking in the Rain' at Sun Studios. Presley never gave a definitive interview during his forty-two years on earth but early in his career he talked about his musical influences. 'Let's face it, nobody can sing that kind of music like coloured people. I can't sing it like Fats Domino can. I know that.' In another interview, he said, 'Down in Tupelo, Mississippi, I used to hear Arthur Crudup bang his box the way I do now and I said if I ever got to the place where I could feel all 'ol Arthur felt, I'd be a music man like nobody ever saw.'

In 1956, Presley attended an otherwise segregated charity show and several black newspapers printed photographs of him with B.B. King. One newspaper reported that Presley told him, 'Thanks, man, for all the early lessons you gave me.'

Wright explained that America's white population just hadn't heard the rocking

✦

In June 1956, Elvis publicly violated segregation ordinances by attending the Memphis fairgrounds on 'coloured night'

✦

R&B because that music was played only in black neighbourhoods. Fifties America was segregated. When a TV camera caught black teenager star Frankie Lyman dancing with a white girl at a music show, several Southern affiliated television stations cancelled the show.

In June 1956, Elvis publicly violated segregation ordinances by attending the Memphis fairgrounds on 'coloured night'.

Bono placed Presley in the context of the Civil Rights movement. In *Rolling Stone's* '100 Greatest Artists of All Time', Bono wrote:

I recently met with Coretta Scott King, John Lewis and some of the other leaders of the American civil-rights movement and they reminded me of the cultural apartheid Rock & Roll was up against. I think the hill they climbed would have been much steeper were it not for racial inroads black music was making on white pop culture. The Beatles, the Rolling Stones, Creedence Clearwater Revival, were all introduced to the Blues through Elvis. He was already doing what the civil-rights movement was demanding: breaking down barriers. You don't think of Elvis as political but that is politics: changing the way people see the world.[60]

Why Was the Music Hidden?

While numerous scholarly volumes have extolled the importance of the Mississippi Delta and Chicago's Urban Blues on the imprint of Rock, an equally important link has been neglected and obscured. Morgan Wright explained the reason for this omission. 'When these books describe the "roots" of Rock & Roll, they usually start with the Blues of the 1930s or earlier, artists like Robert Johnson and Charley Patton and make references to Chicago Blues artists like Howling Wolf and Muddy Waters and then jump right up to 1954, completely skipping over the hard rocking sax-based R&B of the period 1948 to 1953.'

Wright clarified why this link has been hidden.

Technology played a fundamental part. RCA Victor introduced a seven-inch, 45 rpm format in 1949 and this quickly took hold as all the other companies copied their lead; the older ten-inch 78 rpm records were replaced with the modern 45 rpm records. By 1951 and 1952, the only promotional demo records that were shipped to

DJs were the newer 45s. Radio stations dropped the old 78 rpm format records which were heavy, cumbersome and broke easily, and they only played the new 45 rpm records. All the early R&B music was only available on 78s but these vinyl recordings had already been dumped by the radio stations.

At the same time, the jukeboxes in wealthier areas were upgraded to play 45s but most R&B records were still only being issued mainly on 78s so they couldn't be heard. R&B records for the black market were still produced on 78s as late as 1959.

Most black families could not afford the new hardware that played the new small 45 rpm discs. R&B records were the last records issued on a doomed format.

Morgan Wright insists that the Rock & Roll beat, when it first emerged in R&B in the late 1940s, mainly came from Black Gospel and Boogie-woogie Blues. An equally influential factor was Jump

> ✦
> Morgan Wright insists that the Rock & Roll beat, when it first emerged in R&B in the late 1940s, mainly came from Black Gospel and Boogie-woogie Blues
> ✦

Blues since it covered the gap between Swing and Rock & Roll while relying heavily on a swinging saxophone. In a 1990 interview, Little Richard offered this explanation for the birth of rock, 'I would say that boogie-woogie and R&B mixed is Rock & Roll.'

Rock & Roll took off like a rocket and the record companies scrambled to find someone to compete, someone to sell. RCA had Elvis, Decca had Bill Haley and Buddy Holly, Capitol had Gene Vincent. It was clearly not in their interest to re-issue recordings they already had of the earlier R&B musicians since their focus had to be on the 'product' of their latest artists. Fats Domino was one of the exceptions; his first smash was in 1949 a reworking of Champion Jack Dupree's 'Junker's Blues' called 'The Fat Man', and the hits kept coming.

As rock developed, the guitar became the primary instrument to be used and understandably guitarists picked up clues from other guitarists; Eric Clapton looked to B.B. King, while Keith Richards turned to Muddy Waters.

However, prior to 1954, Rock & Roll was saxophone-based, backed up by a boogie-woogie piano. After 1956, the saxophone-led rhythms gave way to the guitar. And all the 1950s' Rock & Roll and R&B stars acknowledged that T-Bone Walker was the inventor of the modern Rock & Roll guitar style.

Faded Stars

For many, Elvis Presley, Chuck Berry, Little Richard, Bill Haley, Jerry Lee Lewis . . . invented Rock & Roll.

But explorers that embarked on a journey of musical discovery have unearthed numerous important characters in this hidden landscape of rock. Some little known, such as Goree Carter and Cecil Gant, others were like Louis Jordan, a genuine superstar with more hits than Chuck Berry and Little Richard together.

The early R&B artists that had influenced and defined the new phase of Rock & Roll faded into oblivion. Today, Louis Jordan, Wynonie Harris, Amos Milburn, T-Bone Walker, Big Joe Turner – among others, are forgotten giants from an age past. Even the Rock and Roll Hall of Fame did not induct Louis Jordan until 1987. He died in 1975.

Internet websites can spread the news, but fuzzy images on YouTube and sepia-tinted photographs captured on eBay listings are all that's left. These are the snapshots of memory, the remnants of the authentic pioneers of Rock & Roll.

The Spirituals and the Blues, the music of the slaves of Africa, inspired and influenced today's modern music and every popular tradition that has emerged since the slave ships landed in America.

This is the – secret – history of Rock & Roll.

♦   ♦   ♦

In the following Photographic Section the images are all numbered and they are described fully in the Photographic Descriptions section starting on page 198.

1. Josiah Henson and his second wife Nancy Gambril.

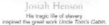

2. Josiah Henson featured on a Canadian stamp.

3. A freed slave in New Orleans.

4. An example of a badge used by slave hunters.

5. A 'slave shop' in Confederate territory during the American Civil War.

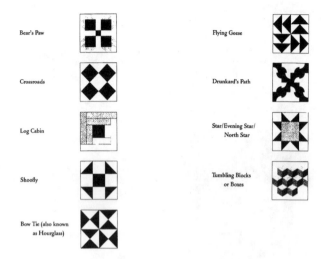

Bear's Paw		Flying Geese	
Crossroads		Drunkard's Path	
Log Cabin		Star/Evening Star/ North Star	
Shoofly		Tumbling Blocks or Boxes	
Bow Tie (also known as Hourglass)			

6. The secret code of the quilt patterns.

7. Wanted poster for Harriet Jacobs.

8. Advertisement for Runaways, 1814.

9. Poster advertising sale of slaves, 1829.

10. Canvas portrait of runaway slave Harriet Tubman from Maryland.

11. Harriet Tubman (far left), with her husband, Nelson Davies (seated).

12. Frederick Douglass.

13. Concert poster for the Jubilee Singers.

14. First day covers in honour of W.C. Handy.

15. Poster for Okeh Records.

16. Mamie Smith.

17. Segregation photo of Coca Cola vending machine.

18. Demonstrators object to African Americans in their white neighbourhood.

19. T-Bone Walker playing the guitar behind his back.

20. Poster advertising Blind Willie Johnson on Columbia Race Records.

21. An advert for Louis Jordan.

Photograph Descriptions

The images in the Photographic Section are all numbered and these are the full descriptions.

1. Josiah Henson and his second wife Nancy Gambril. Henson was sold three times before he reached the age of eighteen. He escaped by following the North Star. When Henson went to the World's Fair in London, he became the first ex-slave to be granted an audience with Queen Victoria. He is thought to be the model for Uncle Tom in Harriet Beecher Stowe's antislavery novel Uncle Tom's Cabin.

2. Josiah Henson was the first black person to be featured on a Canadian stamp in 1983, the centenary of his death.

3. This photograph shows a freed slave who returned to the slave market in New Orleans where she had been sold as a child. The sign on the building reads M. Barnett, Office 40 St Louis Street. The inscription on the card states, 'The Old Slave Block in the Old St Louis Hotel, New Orleans, La. The colored woman standing on the block was sold for $1500.00 on this same block when a little girl.'

4. This badge is sold by collectors as an example of identification used by slave hunters that patrolled plantations to track down runaway slaves.

5. This photograph from the Civil War shows Whitehall Street, Atlanta, Georgia, with a man sitting in front of a building with a shop sign advertising 'Auction & Negro Sales'. The man is probably a Union African-American soldier and his rifle can be seen resting upright next to him. This is one of the rare photographs to show a 'slave shop' in Confederate territory during the Civil War. The photographer has captured the silence of the city with the lone sentry in the city's abandoned street. The street is deserted and researchers have speculated that this view was taken after General William T. Sherman ordered the city to be abandoned in September 1864, but before it was burned in November. The photograph was taken by George Barnard between September and November 1864. It is from the series '3608. The Slave Market, Atlanta, Georgia. The War for the Union. Photographic History.' Courtesy Schomburg Centre, New York Public Library.

6. The secret code of quilt patterns. In 1998 the book, *Hidden in Plain View: A Secret Story of Quilts and the Underground Railroad*, reported that about seventeen slave quilt patterns carried hidden messages for African-American slaves trying to make their way north to freedom. The authors of the book, Jacqueline Tobin and Raymond Dobard, put forward the theory that different quilt patterns were given hidden meanings and that the slaves committed them to memory.

The authors stated that the slaves would sew the patterns and quilts and, as they did so, reinforce the message. The book suggests that the 'Flying Geese' pattern was used to remind escaping slave to follow the geese migrating north.

This theory is disputed by some historians who have been reluctant to accept the accuracy of the secret quilt code because of the lack of documentary evidence. They discount the corroborating information, largely from oral traditions, related by Tobin and Dobard that support the idea.

Courtesy Tobin, J., and Dobard R., *Hidden in Plain View: A Secret Story of Quilts and the Underground Railroad* (Bantam Doubleday, 1999).

7. Wanted poster for Harriet Jacobs. Courtesy Harriet Jacobs Papers Project, Pace University.

8. Advertisement for Runaways from *The United States Gazette*, 1 June 1814. Two adverts: Fifty Dollars Reward and 200 Dollars Reward.

9. Poster advertising the sale of slaves, 1829.

10. Harriet Tubman was a runaway slave from Maryland who led hundreds of salves to freedom at great personal risk. Celebrated for her remarkable exploits, this outstanding heroine is remembered as one of America's most important figures. Slaveholders sought her capture and offered rewards from $12,000 to $40,000 (apparently the total of all rewards put forward). Courtesy United States Library of Congress.

11. Harriet Tubman (far left) with her husband, Nelson Davis (seated, with pipe and walking stick). This was taken in her home where she took in destitute people. Courtesy Schomburg Centre for Research in Black Culture.

12. Frederick Douglass rose from slavery to become the most important African-American voice of the nineteenth century. He was a brilliant speaker with a charismatic presence. Douglass was one of the foremost leaders of the abolitionist movement, which fought to end slavery within the United States in the decades prior to the Civil War. He served as a special advisor to President Abraham Lincoln and his home in Washington has been designated as a National Historic Site. Photograph by George K. Warren about 1879, Courtesy The United States National Archives and Records Administration.

13. This advertisement promoted another sold-out concert for the Jubilee Fisk Singers at Manchester's Town Hall.

14. W.C. Handy named the music he heard 'the Blues'. These three first day covers were issued in 1969 to honour Handy in conjunction with the 150th annversary of the city of Memphis, Tennessee. The Fleetwood cover is signed by the stamp designer, Bernice Kochan. Courtesy United States Postal Service.

15. Record companies marketed speciality labels of 'race records' by and for African-American audiences. This poster was produced for Okeh Records, started in 1918. The company had a surprise smash hit with Mamie Smith, the first Blues record by a black artist. Okeh recorded many classic Jazz performances by artists such as King Oliver, Sidney Bechet and Louis Armstrong. Courtesy Frank Driggs Collection.

16. Mamie Smith was the first to record a song with Blues in its title on Okeh Records. It created a sensation

and sent record companies scrambling to find other female Blues singers who could match the sales of 'Crazy Blues'.

17. Segregation photograph of a Coca Cola vending machine with a sign stating 'white customers only'. After slavery was abolished in the United States, racial discrimination was controlled by the Jim Crow Laws, which implemented strict legalized segregation of the races. Treated as second-class citizens, blacks were separated from whites by law and by private action in transportation, public accommodation, recreational facilities, prisons, armed forces and schools in both northern and southern States.

Beyond the law, however, there was always the threat of terrorist violence against blacks in the South who attempted to challenge, or even question, the established order. The Ku Klux Klan, the Knights of the White Camellia and other terrorist organizations murdered thousands of blacks and some whites in order to prevent them from voting and participating in public life.

Between 1884 and 1900, white mobs lynched more than 2,000 blacks in the South. During World War I (1914–1918), lynching decreased slightly, but between 1900 and 1920 southern whites lynched more than 1,000 blacks. Some were allegedly criminals, but blacks were also lynched for any violation of the code of southern race relations, such as talking to a white woman, attempting to vote, or seeming to make trouble. Lynch mobs not only hanged blacks but also burned them alive, shot them or just beat them to death.

America's last mass lynching occurred on 25 July 1946 when a mob shot two black couples in Walton County, Georgia. The story became national news but no one was ever charged with the murders.

18. African Americans faced protest, intimidation and racist violence if they moved into white neighbourhoods.

19. T-Bone walker playing the guitar behind his back while doing the splits. Walker told audiences that he used to lead Blind Lemon Jefferson around to bars and juke joints to play the Blues. Walker pioneered the electric guitar sound that helped create the modern Blues and set the precedent for everyone that followed. He played one of the first electric guitars in the mid-1930s and pioneered the guitar sound that influenced virtually every guitar player since then, including Chuck Berry, B.B. King, Jimi Hendrix, Stevie Ray Vaughan and Eric Clapton.

20. Poster advertising Columbia Race Records and Blind Willie Johnson. The amazing emotional intensity of Blind Willie Johnson's singing inspired critics and fans to call him the greatest Blues singer in the history of recorded Blues, even though his 30 sides for Columbia between 1927–1930 were all spirituals. His masterpiece 'Dark Was the Night, Cold Was the Ground', was hailed by Ry Cooder as 'the most soulful, transcendent piece in all American music.' It was included on a phonograph recording as part of a variety of sounds and images selected to portray the diversity of life and culture on Planet Earth and carried on board the Voyager spacecraft, launched into space in 1977.

   Johnson was apparently blinded at seven years old, when his stepmother threw lye in his face in revenge after being beaten by his father. As a child, he would be left on street corners to sing for money. Johnson's 78 rpm recording 'If I Had My Way' backed with 'Mother's Children Have a Hard Time' (decades later, Eric Clapton called it 'Motherless Children'), sold a remarkable 15,000 copies, equal to Bessie Smith's recordings of the day. Like most of the other musicians of the period, he would have received a one-off payment of $25 to $50 for each side with the company owning the rights.

Johnson's home burned down in 1945 but, with nowhere else to go, he slept on a wet bed in the ruins. He caught pneumonia two weeks later and died. Afterwards, his wife said that she had tried to admit him to hospital, but he was refused entry because he was black.

His songs have been covered by Bob Dylan, Led Zeppelin, Grateful Dead and The White Stripes, among others.

21. Louis Jordan advert. Louis Jordan has been called the undisputed champion of the Jump Blues movement. Jordan was the crucial link between Big Band Swing and early Rhythm & Blues to the Rock & Roll sound of people like Little Richard, who adopted 'Keep a-Knockin' from Jordan's repertoire. Chuck Berry said simply, 'I identify myself with Louis Jordan more than any other artist,' and Ray Charles acknowledged his debt by signing Jordan to his own Tangerine label in the early 1960s. Jordan launched 54 singles into the R&B charts in the 40s including 18 songs that went to No. 1 – he had more hits than Little Richard and Chuck Berry together.

Endnotes

[1] Douglass, F., *A Narrative of the Life of Frederick Douglass, An American Slave*, Classic Slave Narratives (Longman, 2005).

[2] The year the British MP, William Wilberforce, pushed through his 'Abolition of the Shipping Trade' Act that was the first step to the final end of slavery, which came some years later, in 1838.

[3] Eleven years later, the decision was overturned, as the 14th Amendment of the United States Constitution guaranteed full rights and citizenship, regardless of race.

[4] Henson, J., *Truth Stranger Than Fiction: Father Henson's Story of His Own Life*, 1789–1883. © 2000. This work is the property of the University of North Carolina at Chapel Hill. Acknowledged with thanks.

[5] Henson, J., *The Life of Josiah Henson, Formerly a Slave, Now an Inhabitant of Canada, as Narrated by Himself* (Boston: Arthur D. Phelps, 1849).

[6] Orlando Patterson, *Time Magazine*, 26 April 2007.

[7] Hitchens, C., on Thomas Jefferson, *Sunday Times*, 11 March 2007.

[8] Walvin, J., *Atlas of Slavery* (Pearson Longman, 2006).

[9] Douglass, F., *A Narrative of the Life of Frederick Douglass, An American Slave*, Classic Slave Narratives.

[10] Stroyer, J., *My Life in the South* (Salem: Observer Book and Job Print, 1890).

[11] Bial, R., *The Underground Railroad* (Houghton Mifflin, 2000).

[12] Brown, J., *Slave Life in Georgia: A Narrative of the Life, Sufferings and Escape of John Brown, a Fugitive Slave, Now in England* (Xerox University Microfilms, 1975).

[13] Selected material from the Rice C. Ballard Papers and the Hayes Collection Southern Historical Collection, Wilson Library, The University of North Carolina at Chapel Hill.

[14] Hurmence, B., Ed., *Before Freedom: When I Just Can Remember* (John F. Blair, 1989). The United States Library of Congress, home of the Slave Narratives Collection. Acknowledged with thanks.

[15] Historical Collections of Ohio, *Ohio Before the Civil War* (AzArrow, 2007).

[16] Bial, R., *The Underground Railroad*.

[17] Tobin, R. and R. Dobard, *Hidden in Plain View: A Secret Story of Quilts and the Underground Railroad* (Bantam Doubleday, 1999).

[18] Blockson, C.L., *The Underground Railroad* (Prentice Hall Press, 1987).

[19] Blight, C., *Passages to Freedom* (Smithsonian Books, 2004).

[20] Bial, R., *The Underground Railroad*.

[21] Still, W., *Underground Railroad*, 1872 (from Project Gutenberg).

[22] Sterling, D., *Freedom Train – The Story of Harriet Tubman* (Scholastic, 1987).

[23] Clinton, C., *Harriet Tubman: The Road to Freedom* (Back Bay Books, Little Brown and Company, 2005).

[24] Douglass, F., *A Narrative of the Life of Frederick Douglass, An American Slave*, Classic Slave Narratives.

[25] Pennington, J., *The Fugitive Blacksmith or Events in the History of James W.C. Pennington* (Cornell University Library, 1849).

[26] Jacobs, H., *Incidents in the Life of a Slave Girl* (Dover Publications, 2001).

27 Blight, D., *Passages to Freedom: The Underground Railroad in History and Memory* (Smithsonian Books, 2006).

28 Still, W., *Underground Railroad*, 1872.

29 Gorrell, G., *North Star to Freedom* (Stoddart, 1996).

30 Bordewich, F., *Bound for Canaan* (Amistad Press, 2006).

31 Coffin, L., *Reminiscence* (Robert Clarke, 1875).

32 Quadroons were a quarter Negro; octoroons were an eighth.

33 Equiano, O., *The Interesting Narrative of the Life of Olaudah Equiano, or Gustavus Vassa, the African* (Random House, 2004).

34 Mariners' Museum, *Captive Passage: The Transatlantic Slave Trade and the Making of the Americas*: Heywood's chapter, 'The African Diaspora: Resistance and Survival' (Smithsonian Books, 2002).

35 *Slave Songs of the United States* 1867 (Oak, 1965).

36 Hochschild, A., *Bury the Chains* (Pan, 2006).

37 Schama, S., *Rough Crossings* (London: BBC Books, 2006).

38 Gorrell, G., *North Star to Freedom*.

39 Dodson, H., *Jubilee: The Emergence of African-American Culture* (Diane Publishing, 2003).

40 Walker, D., *Appeal to the Coloured Citizens of the World* (Pennsylvania State University Press, 2000).

41 Gorrell, G., *North Star to Freedom*.

42 Dvořák, A., 'Music in America', *Harper's New Monthly Magazine* (Feb. 1895), with the co-operation of Mr Edwin Emerson Jr.

43 Anderson, M., *My Lord, What a Morning* (New York: The Viking Press, 1956).

44 Handy, W.C., *The Father of the Blues* (Jazz Book Club, Sidgwick and Jackson, 1961).

45 Handy, W.C., *The Father of the Blues*.

46 Garofalo, R., *Split Images: African-Americans in the Mass Media* (Howard University Press, 1990).

47 Springer, R., *Nobody Knows Where the Blues Come From: Lyrics and History* (University Press of Mississippi, 2005).

48 George-Warren, H., Ed., C.J. Farley, R. Santelli and P. Guralnick, *Martin Scorsese Presents The Blues, A Musical Journey* (HarperCollins/Amistad, 2003).

49 Santelli, R., *The Big Book of Blues: A Biographical Encyclopedia* (Penguin, 2001).

50 Hamilton, M., *In Search of the Blues* (Jonathan Cape, 2007).

51 Scaruffi, P., *A Brief History of Popular Music Before Rock Music* (iUniverse.com, 2003).

52 Merlis, B., and Davin Seay, *Heart and Soul* (Verve Editions, 2004).

53 Warner, J., *Just Walking in the Rain* (Renaissance Books, 2001).

54 Hamilton, M., *In Search of the Blues*.

55 Marsh D., *Alan Lomax*: *Dead, But Still Stealing*, www.counterpunch.org.

56 Malan, R., article on Solomon Linda appeared in *Rolling Stone* magazine in 2002.

57 Millen, G., on Memphis www.americanheritage.com.

58 Wright, M., www.hoyhoy.com.

59 Rothwell, F., *Long Distance Information: Chuck Berry's Recorded Legacy* (Music Mentor Books, 2001).

60 'Bono on Elvis Presley, The Immortals: The First Fifty, The Fifty Great Artists of All Time' www.rollingstone.com.

Bibliography

Resistance

Blassingame, J., *The Slave Community* (New York: Oxford University Press, 1972).

Blockson, C.L., 'The Underground Railroad', *National Geographic Magazine* (July 1984).

Martin, S.I., *Britain's Slave Trade* (London: Channel 4 Books, 1999).

Plimmer, C. and D., *Slavery: The Anglo-American Involvement* (New York: Barnes & Noble, 1973).

Smith, D., *Slavery Now and Then* (Eastbourne: Kingsway, 2007).

Thomas, H., *The Slave Trade* (London: Picador, 1997).

Wolny, P., *The Underground Railroad* (New York: Rosen, 2004).

Africans in America, Public Broadcasting Service: www.pbs.org.

National Underground Railroad Freedom Center: www.freedomcenter.org.

Legacy

Barker, H. and Y. Taylor, *Faking It: The Quest for Authenticity in Popular Music* (London: Faber and Faber, 2007).

Rolf, J., Gen. Ed., *Blues: The Complete Story* (London: Flame Tree, 2007).

Clarke, D., *The Rise and Fall of Popular Music* (London: Viking, 1995).

Dates, J. and W. Barlow, *Split Image: African Americans in the Mass Media* (Washington, DC: Howard University Press, 1990).

Fisher, M.M., *Negro Slave Songs in the United States* (California: Citadel Press, reissue ed. 1991).

Garofalo, R., *Crossing Over: From Rhythm & Blues to Rock & Roll. Rhythm and Business: The Political Economy of Black Music*, Ed. by N. Kelley (New York: Akashic Books, 2005).

Oliver, P., *The Story of the Blues* (London: Penguin Books, 1972).

Rolling Stone Illustrated History of Rock & Roll, The (London: Random House/Rolling Stone, 1980).

Southern, E., *The Music of Black Americans: A History* (New York: Norton, 1971).

Thomas, V.M., *No Man Can Hinder Me* (London: Random House, 2001).

Bill Hampson

Bill Hampson is a Deputy Lieutenant of Greater Manchester and has been a leading campaigner for human rights for many years. He first met and worked with Danny Smith in Jubilee Campaign's most formative years and was made a Freeman of Wigan in 2000 for his charity work, particularly in bringing together churches, local authority and voluntary organizations from around the area, to provide aid, support and development work in Romania after the fall of communism.

As a founding Director of the Epiphany Trust, he has developed a range of high class projects in Romania, Sri Lanka, Burma and other parts of South Asia; as well as Chrysalis Holidays which is a social enterprise in Greater Manchester providing educational holidays for adults with learning disabilities.

Bill, formerly a surveyor, currently sits on the boards of the Wigan Leisure & Culture Trust which runs all cultural and leisure services within the borough, Global Hand and Jigsaw 4U International, a bereavement counselling service for children.

Married to Pam, he is also President of Lowton Independent Methodist Church.

The Epiphany Trust

The Epiphany Trust is dedicated to helping others, regardless of creed or culture, by aid and education, and by encouraging groups and individuals wishing to initiate or continue their own projects. The Trust seeks in particular to serve the needs of disabled and disadvantaged people and those who support them.

The Epiphany Trust currently has projects in Albania, Burma, Democratic Republic of Congo, Pakistan, Romania, Sri Lanka and the UK.

The Epiphany Trust, St David's, Park Road South, Newton-le-Willows, Merseyside, WA12 8EY. Tel 01925 220999 or bill@epiphany.org.uk www.epiphany.org.uk.

Danny Smith

Danny Smith is married to Joan and lives in Surrey. They have three children – Rachel, Luke and Jessica, who passed away unexpectedly in December 2007, an event Danny describes as 'traumatic and transforming'.

An Anglo Indian, Danny made his career in journalism, media and communications. With a life-long interest in music, he has interviewed Mahalia Jackson, Little Richard, Bob Dylan, Joan Baez and Peter, Paul and Mary, among others. His mentors include George Verwer of Operation Mobilisation, and Peter Benenson, the founder of Amnesty International. His strategic influence has shaped Danny's life's work and the direction of Jubilee Campaign – launched in Parliament by David Alton in 1987.

Danny has led numerous successful campaigns including winning freedom for the 'Siberian Seven'; a change in the law to prosecute British sex tourists who travel abroad to abuse children and a 'Kids Behind Bars' campaign (with Fr Shay Cullen) which resulted in changes in the law in the Philippines.

At the forefront of clandestine work in Ceausescu's Romania, Danny helped Olivia Harrison and the wives of the Beatles to establish the Romanian Angel Appeal in

1989 and served this pioneering work as a trustee. In 2005, he delivered the keynote address at the graduation service at the Handong International Law School in South Korea; Lord Janner acclaimed his book on Raoul Wallenberg, *Lost Hero,* and declared 'it should be compulsory reading in all our schools'.

Danny's mission now is to concentrate on a charitable tribute to Jessica in India, the Philippines and Zimbabwe, and to develop Jubilee Campaign's future direction as it combines effective lobbying with dynamic practical help for children at risk worldwide.

danny@jubileecampaign.co.uk

Jubilee Campaign

Jubilee Campaign is an effective human rights pressure group that tackles the causes of injustice and has been successful at bringing real and lasting change for children at risk and persecuted Christian families worldwide.

Jubilee Campaign was awarded consultative status at the United Nations and helped to set up the All Party Parliamentary Group on Street Children, serving as its secretariat since its inception in 1992.

New charitable laws in the UK have made it possible for Jubilee Campaign to extend its mission and secure charitable status to provide direct practical help where it will really make a difference and change more lives. This important development will enable Jubilee Campaign to work in strategic partnerships with people such as Fr Shay Cullen's Preda Foundation in the Philippines, and Reverend K.K. Devaraj's Bombay Teen Challenge in India.

Jubilee Campaign, PO Box 700, Addlestone, Surrey
KT15 9BW Tel 01200 430430
www.jubileecampaign.co.uk
info@jubileecampaign.co.uk